Who's Afraid of John Maynard Keynes?

"Paul Davidson is the keeper of the Keynesian flame. Keynes lives (intellectually), and Davidson is one of the reasons."
—Alan S. Blinder, *Gordon S. Rentschler Memorial Professor of Economics and Public Affairs, Princeton University, USA*

Paul Davidson

Who's Afraid of John Maynard Keynes?

Challenging Economic Governance in an Age of Growing Inequality

Paul Davidson
Holly Chair of Excellence Emeritus
University of Tennessee at Knoxville
Knoxville, TN, USA

ISBN 978-3-319-64503-2   ISBN 978-3-319-64504-9 (eBook)
DOI 10.1007/978-3-319-64504-9

Library of Congress Control Number: 2017950681

© The Editor(s) (if applicable) and The Author(s) 2017
This work is subject to copyright. All rights are solely and exclusively licensed by the Publisher, whether the whole or part of the material is concerned, specifically the rights of translation, reprinting, reuse of illustrations, recitation, broadcasting, reproduction on microfilms or in any other physical way, and transmission or information storage and retrieval, electronic adaptation, computer software, or by similar or dissimilar methodology now known or hereafter developed.
The use of general descriptive names, registered names, trademarks, service marks, etc. in this publication does not imply, even in the absence of a specific statement, that such names are exempt from the relevant protective laws and regulations and therefore free for general use.
The publisher, the authors and the editors are safe to assume that the advice and information in this book are believed to be true and accurate at the date of publication. Neither the publisher nor the authors or the editors give a warranty, express or implied, with respect to the material contained herein or for any errors or omissions that may have been made. The publisher remains neutral with regard to jurisdictional claims in published maps and institutional affiliations.

Cover credit: Chronicle/Alamy Stock Photo

Printed on acid-free paper

This Palgrave Macmillan imprint is published by Springer Nature
The registered company is Springer International Publishing AG
The registered company address is: Gewerbestrasse 11, 6330 Cham, Switzerland

Foreword

In a 1936 book entitled *The General Theory of Employment Interest and Money*, John Maynard Keynes developed a revolutionary general theory to explain the cause of the Great Depression and suggest what policies government can undertake to end the existence of persistent high levels of unemployment. Keynes wrote "this book is chiefly addressed to my fellow economists [to tell them that the orthodox classical theory was at] fault, in a lack of clearness and of generality in its premises."[1] Keynes indicated that his general theory's conclusions were "in contrast...with those of the *classical* theory...[where] the postulates of the classical theory are applicable to a special case...[that] happen[s] not to be...the economic society in which we actually live, with the result that its teaching is misleading and disastrous if we attempt to apply it to the facts of experience."[2]

After the Second World War, economic textbooks devoted several chapters to a macroeconomic theory that was called "Keynesian" theory, although the microfoundations of this mainstream "Keynesian" theory was based on classical economic theory. Joan Robinson, a famous economist who was a student of Keynes in the 1930s called this mainstream "Keynesian" theory "Bastard Keynesianism" since it attempted to merge classical theory of individual decision-making in the marketplace with some macroeconomic terminology developed by Keynes.

For more than four decades, in professional articles and books that I have written, I have been trying to convince mainstream economists in academia that what they have been teaching as "Keynesian" economics was not the general theory developed by John Maynard Keynes in his 1936 book. I have stressed that mainstream "Keynesian" macroeconomics has as its microfoundation classical theory—typically a mathematical form of classical theory called general equilibrium theory. Consequently, policy implications developed from this "Bastard Keynesianism" often produced, as Keynes said classical theory would, misleading and sometimes disastrous results. This has become more obvious with the global financial crisis of 2007–2008 and the Great Recession that has lasted almost a decade since the onset of this global financial crisis.

In 1994, I wrote a textbook that I addressed to my fellow economists and their students entitled Post Keynesian Macroeconomic Theory to contrast the technical aspects of classical-based "Keynesian" theory with the development of a Post Keynesian analysis that brings Keynes's original general theory up-to-date in explaining the operation of modern money using, market-oriented economies. Although this textbook has gone through two editions and continues to sell, I found that mainstream economists, including government economic advisors, central bankers, and economists at many financial enterprises were not ready to accept this Keynes-Post Keynesian analysis. Instead, they still use some variant of the false "Bastard Keynesian" theory. The result has been that many government economic policies have not solved the economic problems we have experienced and some policies often have made things appear to be worse.

Moreover, as I note in Chap. 2 of this book, in Congressional testimony, mainstream economist Former Federal Reserve Chairman Alan Greenspan stated he was shocked in disbelief when the global financial crisis occurred in 2007 and this event has caused the entire "intellectual edifice" of mainstream macroeconomic theory to "collapse."

When I read that Queen Elizabeth of Great Britain had asked economists at the London School of Economics why nobody had seen the development of the global financial crisis and then I read the foolish answer the queen received, I thought the time was ripe to write a book aimed at my fellow economists to explain, in some technical detail, how Keynes-Post Keynesian theory provided a factual explanation of the cause of the global financial crisis. My book would also provide evidence that, several years before the crisis, I had warned, in print, of the coming of a financial crisis. This book was entitled *Post Keynesian Theory and Policy*[3] and was published in 2015 by Edward Elgar. Some of the material in this book was included in that volume and I am grateful to Edward Elgar for allowing me to reproduce it here.

In the campaign for nomination for President of the USA, I noted that the potential Presidential candidates failed to provide the public with any correct policies that would solve the global economic problems that we are facing. I decided to rewrite the message of my *Post Keynesian Theory and Policy* in a new book that is stripped of its most technical jargon.

I indicated that I believed that many highly intelligent readers of economic writings that uses technical verbiage regarding models, theories, equations, etc. find such texts uninvitingly dismal and obtuse. I wanted to present the Post Keynesian policy message in a simple language that the average intelligent layperson can understand rather than providing an explanation in the vocabulary of the professional economist. I suggested that the title for this new book should be *Who's Afraid of John Maynard Keynes?* My hope for this new book was by providing these ideas in a simple exposition, I could educate the voting population to understand the economic problems our economy faces. They could then demand that those running for political office provide economic policies that (a) address directly these understandable economic problems and (b) were capable of developing policies in an understandable manner to assure a prosperous full employment economy.

Knoxville, USA   Paul Davidson

Notes

1. J.M. Keynes, *The General Theory of Employment interest and Money*, (Macmillan, London, 1936) p. V.
2. *Op. cit.*, p. 3.
3. P. Davidson, *Post Keyneian Theory and Policy* (Edwad Elgar, Cheltenham, 2005).

Contents

1   Introduction: Who Saw the Coming of the Global
    Financial Crisis of 2007–2008?   1

2   Alternative Explanations of How the Capitalist Economy
    in Which We Live Operates   7

3   Understanding the Role of Money and Money Contracts
    in a Market Economy   19

4   Unemployment: Why Can't People Who Want to Work
    Find Jobs?   39

5   Creating a Prosperous Full Employment Economy   55

6   Can We Prevent Inflation and Still Achieve Full
    Employment?   63

7   The Role of Financial Markets and Liquidity   81

8	Globalization and International Trade Effects on Employment and Prosperity	97
9	Are Free Trade Agreements Always Beneficial?	127
10	President Trump's Anti-free Trade Agreements Policy	141
11	What Economic Policies Can a Democracy Adopt to Assure We Live in a Prosperous, Civilized Capitalist System?	145
Index		155

1

Introduction: Who Saw the Coming of the Global Financial Crisis of 2007–2008?

On November 4, 2008 at the dedication of a new building, Queen Elizabeth of Great Britain visited the London School of Economics [LSE]. While there she was given a briefing by academics at the LSE on the origins and effects of the global financial crisis and its resulting turmoil in international financial markets. The Queen is reported to have asked "Why did nobody notice it developing?" The director of research at LSE told her "At every stage someone was relying on somebody else and everyone thought they were doing the right thing".

How is it possible that the many intelligent investors, bankers, brokers, fund managers and other financial market participants thought they were doing the right thing, when it is clear from hindsight that financial market activity was creating a situation that ultimately caused global financial markets to collapse and result in the worse global economic performance since the Great Depression? Why did not any of the many Nobel Prize Laureates in Economics warn governments and the public of this forthcoming global economic storm?

The answer lies in the fact that, at least for more than four decades, the mainstream economic theory that has dominated academic teaching, Nobel Laureate research, mainstream professional economic journals

© The Author(s) 2017
P. Davidson, *Who's Afraid of John Maynard Keynes?*,
DOI 10.1007/978-3-319-64504-9_1

and the thoughts of financial market professionals and journalists is not applicable to the economic system in which we live. Nevertheless this dominant mainstream theory's teachings is the foundation of the economic reasoning of economic students who then became bankers, entrepreneurs, politicians, government regulators, central bankers, etc. This mainstream theory, however, is a fairy tale fable that has no descriptive relationship with the operations of our market oriented, money using capitalist economy. Consequently what was seen as a way of doing good in this fairy tale economy, created destructive economic forces in the world in which we live.

There are a few economists, however, that have a better understanding of how the modern market economy works. They did publically warn that financial markets were creating an unstable situation that, sooner or later, was going to cause a terrible financial markets problem. These economists who saw the economic financial crisis coming call themselves Post Keynesians since they used and further developed the general theory that, in 1936, the English economist John Maynard Keynes had originated to explain why the financial crisis recognized by the New York Stock Market collapse in 1929 had created the Great Depression that encompassed the global economic system for years.

As early as 2002, in my Post Keynesian book *Financial markets, money and the real world*.[1] I noted that in our modern market economies, the development of new, organized markets for financial assets was creating a potential economic problem. I noted that the existence of organized financial markets is a potential double-edged sword. The good edge of the sword is that these markets can help savers who currently do not want to spend all their earned income funds to buy producible things to transfer their saving out of current income to others including investors who want to purchase new capital plant and equipment that costs more than the current income these others have earned.

In return for transferring their saving money funds to investors, savers receive financial assets such as stocks, bonds, shares of mutual funds, etc. These financial assets provide a place for savers to store their savings while hopefully earn income from their portfolio of financial assets. These financial assets are considered to be liquid as long as the savers believe that these financial assets can be readily resold in the organized financial market for cash when, any time in the future, the savers wish to make a fast exit from holding these financial assets and return their savings to a cash reserve form which they can then readily spend on anything if they so desire.

This good edge facilitates financing more capital goods investment including very large investment projects—projects often too large to be funded by any single individual or small group of partners. In so doing, the resulting investment projects typically increases productivity and in so doing reduce the costs of producing new goods and services for households to purchase. Thus the lower costs of buying goods make households better off.

The bad edge of these organized financial markets is that, in circumstances when many holders of these liquid financial assets suddenly have increasing fears about what may happen in the uncertain economic future, then the liquidity of financial assets can evaporate as many liquid asset holders rush to sell in the market while potential buyers disappear from these financial markets. The result is the market price of these liquid assets can fall even to zero and thereby result in severe economic liquidity and insolvency problems for the asset holders that can engulf the global financial community.

An illiquid financial asset is a debt or equity certificate for which no market exists where holders of these assets can resell them quickly at a reasonable price. For example the borrower of a bank loan—such as a mortgage loan—may sign a debt certificate, but there is typically no market where this debt certificate can be readily resold for cash. Consequently this bank loan debt certificate in an illiquid financial asset and the holder awaits payments by the borrower to recover the loan plus interest.

When government regulators of financial markets permitted financial institutions to bundle together many illiquid mortgage debts to create mortgage back derivative securities (which encompassed sub prime mortgages[2] in the mix) to profitably sell to savers, the seeds of financial catastrophe were being sowed.[3] Savers were told that these securitized derivatives could be easily resold in organized derivative financial markets, thus convincing buyers that these mortgage backed derivative securities are liquid even though the mortgages underlying these derivatives were illiquid.

This securitization process allowed many risky illiquid subprime mortgages to be bundled together with more illiquid conventional mortgages. This securitized mortgage-back derivative bundling appeared to increase the potential earnings of a portfolio while reducing the risk of an overall bad defaulted portfolio holding by savers since there would still be many in-good standing mortgages in the derivative bundle. Accordingly these derivative securities were considered to be doing a social good in that more subprime mortgage loans could be made to allow many people to buy homes that they otherwise could not afford. Simultaneously, these derivative assets promised saver-holders a larger rate of return than they could obtain by putting their savings elsewhere (e.g., into a money market account or even buying US government bonds)—another apparent good.

Since the investment bank packager of these securitized derivatives typically advertised that these financial assets were "as good as cash" i.e., were readily liquidated for money in the market, the purchasers of these derivatives did not fear any significant loss if, and when, they decided to make a fast exit and sold their holdings of these derivatives for cash. Moreover, rating agencies that profess to provide an objective report to the general public of the credit worthiness of such securitized financial assets gave these mortgage backed derivatives an AAA rating that further encouraged savers to believe that these derivatives were a safe liquid investment for their funds.

No wonder, as the LSE director told the Queen, "everyone thought they were doing the right thing" for themselves and their economic community. But in 2007 these derivative and other new securitized markets appeared to collapse as many holders of these various derivative securities became bearish and suddenly wanted to sell to make a fast exit from the market to obtain cash, while no one apparently wanted to buy these derivatives offered for sale. The result was a liquidity crisis as these derivatives were now recognized as "toxic assets" that lost all market value in the absence of sufficient buyers (bulls) to offset the sellers (bears).

Accounting rules require that securities that are liquid and are held in one's balance sheet must be valued at their current market price on the asset side of the balance sheet. Since these toxic assets were held not only by individuals but also held across the global financial community by bankers, pension funds, other institutional funds, the asset side of the balance sheets of these institutions and individuals collapsed thereby severely damaging or destroying the accounting value of the net worth of the holders of these assets. The resulting financial crisis did not spare any important national economy.

In my 2002 book *Financial markets, money and the real world*, I noted that a financial crisis was likely to occur in the near future. I wrote that in the USA:

> Recent trends in the growth of mutual funds and other nonbank financial intermediaries have encouraged saver households to reallocate their saving portfolio from holding (government insured) bank deposits towards holding more liabilities [issued by] nonbank financial intermediaries. This has permitted a significant expansion of debt obligations on the part of debtor households and enterprises. This suggests that a sudden switch by many [portfolio holding savers] … to a fast exit strategy at a future date could cause a horrific liquidity problem.[4]

The global financial crisis of 2007–2008 indicates how prophetic this 2002 Post Keynesian message proved to be.

As we will discuss in the following chapters, the Post Keynesian analytical system can suggest ways to dull the bad edge of liquid financial markets swords via (1) legislating proper regulatory rules on financial markets and (2) have central banks ready to alleviate a financial liquidity crisis if it still occurs. Accordingly, a major purpose of this book is to explain, not only to Queen Elizabeth but to all, why what is the mainstream's fairy-tale classical economic theory that is still being espoused by the talking head "experts" and "elites" on TV and in governments, central banks and even international institutions such as the International Monetary Fund. In contrast, while, still often ignored, the Post Keynesian approach developed in the following chapters is available to provide a realistic analysis of the operation of the money using capitalist economy in which we live. Once the public understands the operation of a 21st century money using, market oriented world economy as explained by the Keynes—Post Keynesian analysis, then the public can choose government officials who will understand why the policies necessary to deal with economic problems when they occur are significantly different than those often currently espoused by elite experts.

Notes

1. P. Davidson, *Financial Markets, Money and The Real World*, (Elgar, Cheltenham, 2002), chapter. 6.
2. A sub prime mortgage is a loan made to individuals to help purchase a home. These individuals typically are poor credit risks, often are unable to prove income earnings, and posses few, if any, other assets that can be pledged as collateral. The sub prime loan typically involves high origination fees, prepayment penalties, balloon maturities and other costs that make it difficult to refinance the loan if interest rates decline. Often the loan comes with an artificially low introductory rate that ratchets upward substantially thereby increasing monthly payments by as much as 50%. The good was these sub prime loans increased opportunities for home ownership adding nine million US households to be homeowners in the decade from 1996 to 2006. Often this permitted the poor to gain the American Dream of home ownership. The bad is when monthly payments rose on these type of loans the default rate becomes very large.
3. At this point we shall illustrate the problem with the securitization of mortgage back derivative securities. But at the same time, other exotic securities such as credit-default swaps, etc. were being invested and sold to the public which had similar faults.
4. *Op cit.*, p. 117.

2

Alternative Explanations of How the Capitalist Economy in Which We Live Operates

To understand why so many elite talking heads on TV and in the printed media did not see the global financial crisis coming, and why they can not readily explain policies that make prosperity an everlasting property of the economic system in which we live, the reader must first understand that there are two very different explanations (theories) of how the economic system that we call capitalism works. These are: (1) the classical theory and (2) the Keynes–Post Keynesian theory.

Unfortunately, to confuse matters, the classical theory has many sub classifications that go under different names although, as we will explain, all use the basic classical assumptions as their fundamental foundation. The classical theory sub classifications are

(1a) the free market theory as championed by Nobel Prize economists [e.g. Milton Friedman, Robert Lucas] of the University of Chicago,

(1b) Neoclassical Synthesis Keynesianism theory associated with Nobel Prize winning economists [e.g., Paul Samuelson, Robert Solow] of the Massachusetts Institute of Technology, and

(1c)   New Keynesianism theory associated with Nobel Prize winning economists [e.g., Paul Krugman of Princeton University and Joseph Stiglitz of Columbia University].

Advocates of subdivision (1b) and (1c) claim that their theory is developed from the general theory created by the English economist John Maynard Keynes in his 1936 book entitled "The General Theory of Employment Interest and Money". The vast majority of economists who teach in academia and/or who are advisors to governments, central banks, and financial institutions have not read Keynes but still believe these classical subdivisions (1b) and (1c) are accurate representations of Keynes's book. We will show, however, that these classical so called "Keynesian" theories' are built upon assumed foundations that are actually incompatible with Keynes's explanation of the operation of our money using, market oriented economic system.

The acceptance of these classical sub divisions as "Keynesian" theory—although they are not Keynes—have encouraged politicians and governments to adopt policies advocated by these so-called "Keynesians", but these policies have brought about some bad economic outcomes, e.g., stagflation (i.e., price inflation while the economy suffers from high levels of unemployment), outsourcing of domestic jobs under the banner of free trade, and the growing inequality of income and wealth in developed capitalist economies. This increasing inequality has hollowed out the prosperous middle class that had developed since Second World War. As these unfortunate outcomes have been associated with classical "Keynesian" policy advice, consequentially these outcomes have created fear among politicians and ordinary citizens of any policies associated with the name of John Maynard Keynes. Today, almost all politicians are afraid of any policy labelled "Keynesian".

The main purpose of this book is to explain (1) why the Keynes–Post Keynesian explanation of the operation of the monetary, market oriented economic system we call capitalism is more appropriate for understanding the operation of our economic system than either the free market classical theory or any of the aforementioned classical sub class "Keynesian" theories and then (2) to suggest Keynes–Post Keynesian economic policies to remove the flaws in the capitalist system and thereby cure threats of financial crisis, of inflation, the loss of domestic jobs and the growing national inequality of income and wealth.

But first, let us provide a brief Keynes–Post Keynesian explanation of the global financial crisis of 2007–2008 to respond to the query of Queen Elizabeth what caused the financial crisis that apparently no economic advisors to governments saw developing.

The financial crisis that began in 2007–2008 started as a small default problem on some subprime mortgages that had been issued in the United States. These defaulting sub prime mortgages were part of the mix of created derivative securities that are known as mortgage backed derivatives. Holders of these derivative securities could neither easily discern how much of the mix of mortgages underlying their securities were sub prime mortgages nor who were the actual borrowers of all the mortgages or the value of the houses being mortgage financed that made up the mix underlying their particular derivative securities.

When the sub prime mortgage borrowers in the mix of some of these derivative securities began to default, the holders of all this complex derivative securities began to fear that the mortgages in their specific derivative security holdings might also soon fall into default. Consequently many derivative asset holders tried to sell their securities in order to make fast exits from the markets for these derivative assets as the fear of potential defaults spread. With derivative holders rushing to exit the derivative securities market while practically no one were willing to buy more of these derivative securities, the market prices of these derivatives crashed.

The accepted accounting rule required liquid assets held in one's portfolio be "marked to market", i.e., the balance sheet valuation of these securities are determined by their market price. When the market price of mortgage backed derivatives crashed, the result was to collapse the value of the asset side of balance sheets of all individuals and institutions that held these derivatives, threatening these holders with potential insolvency or even worse.

This effect quickly ballooned globally into the largest threat to economic prosperity since the Great Depression. What is rarely noted is that the origin of this latest global financial market crisis, like the New

York Stock exchange crash of 1929 that appears to have precipitated the Great Depression, is associated with the loss of market value of securities operation in free financial markets unhampered by government regulations.

In recent decades, many mainstream academic economists, central bankers such as Alan Greenspan, as well as most policy makers in government and their economic advisors have advocated freeing financial markets from government rules and regulators. These free market advocates insist that

1. government regulation of markets and large government spending policies are the cause of our economic problems,
2. market participants have their own self-interest in mind and therefore they "know" how to behave in these free markets to optimize their position and therefore
3. ending big government and freeing markets from regulatory controls are the solutions to our economic problems.

In an amazing "mea culpa" testimony before the House Committee on Oversight and Government Reform on October 23, 2008, Alan Greenspan, the former Chair of the Federal Reserve System and a strong advocate of unregulated free markets, admitted that he had overestimated the ability of free financial markets to self correct any problems that may occur. Greenspan indicated that he had entirely missed the possibility that deregulation could unleash a destructive force on the economy. In his testimony regarding the onset of the global financial crisis, Greenspan stated:

> "This crisis, however, has turned out to be much broader than I could have imagined…those of us who had looked to the self interest of lending institutions to protect shareholders' equity (myself especially) are in a state of shocked disbelief.…In recent decades a vast risk management and pricing system has evolved, combining the best insights of mathematicians and finance experts supported by major advances in computer and communications technology. A Nobel Prize [in economics] was awarded for the discovery of the [free market] pricing model that underpins much

of the advance in [financial] derivatives markets. This modern risk management paradigm held sway for decades. The whole intellectual edifice, however, collapsed."

Under questioning by members of the House Oversight and Government Reform Committee, Greenspan admitted "I found a flaw in the models that I perceive is the critical functioning structure that defines how the world works. That's precisely the reason I was shocked... I still do not fully understand why it happened, and obviously to the extent that I figure it happened and why, I shall change my views".

In other words, Greenspan has noted that free financial markets do not function as his classical theory says they should. We shall explain to Greenspan and other elites the flaw in their classical theory explaining the "functioning structure" of the world market economic and financial system works.

Theory Provides Explanation

Since biblical times, humans have tried to understand the things they observe happening around them. In general, the human mind believes that there must be a cause for any event we observe. For most of the history of mankind, human belief attributed to the design of God or the Gods as the cause of anything that happened.

In the seventeenth century, philosophers began to argue that explanations of observed events could be developed on the basis of reasoning of the mind. In this intellectual movement that historians called the Age of Reason or Enlightenment, order and regularity was seen to come from human analysis of observed phenomena. The power of truth was not in the possession of truth but in its acquisition. The goal was to understand and explain observed processes occurring in our world.

To this end, it was essential to develop theories that would explain observed phenomena. Any understanding of the world we observe will be the creation of the human mind. Reasoning involves the mind creating a theory to explain what people observe happening. A theory is essentially the way humans attempt to explain observed phenomena on the basis of a logical model that is built on the foundation of some fundamental axioms (presumptions). An axiom is an assumption that the theorist model builder accepts as a self evident universal truth that does not have to be proven. From this axiomatic assumptions foundation, the theorist uses the laws of logic to build a theory that reaches one or more conclusions.

In economics these conclusions are presented to the public as the explanation of economic events that are occurring, or will occur, in our world of experience. The theory is then used to suggest what can, or cannot be done, to affect future economic outcomes. If the facts of experience conflict with what are the logical conclusions of one's economic theory, as Greenspan admits happened in his theory of free financial markets, then one or more of the theory's fundamental axioms are flawed. The theory is unrealistic and should be discarded in order to permit a different—more realistic—theory to be built. The alternative to developing a better theory would be to change the facts—or even one's definition of the facts—to fit the unrealistic theory.[1]

No theory is ever accepted as the final explanation of observed events. Rather theories are accepted until they are supplanted by "better" theories. Typically the better theory requires fewer restrictive axioms for its foundation than the older theory it replaces.

One can consider the builder of any economic theory as if he/she is a magician. Theorists rarely make logical errors in moving from axioms to conclusions any more than a professional prestidigitator drops the deck of cards while performing a card trick. Most economics theorists are proficient at creating the illusion of pulling policy conclusion rabbits out of their black hat model of the operation of the economy. Often the policy rabbits pulled from the black hat model generates some audience enjoyment and applause.

A careful examination of the [axiomatic] rabbits the magician [economic theorist] put initially into the black hat back stage is required to evaluate the relevance of the policy rabbits pulled from the black hat on stage. Before accepting the logical conclusions of any economic theory as correct and therefore applicable to our money using, market oriented economic system, central bankers such as Alan Greenspan, government officials, business executives, politicians and the general public should examine and be prepared to question the fundamental assumptions of any theory. If these assumptions are not applicable to our economic world, then the policy conclusions of this theory must be rejected as irrelevant and even possibly harmful.

Alternative Theories

There are two fundamental economic theories that attempt to explain the operation of the market oriented, money using, capitalist economy in which we live-classical theory and Keynes-Post Keynesian theory. The classical economic theory that has tended to reign supreme in mainstream economic circles since the latter part of the eighteenth century. There are many versions of this classical theory that go under different names but all are based on some of the same fundamental assumption foundation. The labels for these versions include efficient market theory, Walrasian theory, general equilibrium theory, dynamic general equilibrium theory, Austrian theory *and* mainstream "Keynesian" theories including the neoclassical synthesis Keynesian theory developed by Nobel Prize winner Paul Samuelson and the New Keynesian theory developed by students of the Samuelson neoclassical synthesis Keynesian approach. The proponents of these variants of the classical axiomatic analysis may differ on the details of their analysis but the mantra of all these approaches is that, in the long run, if markets possess freely flexible wages and product prices, then these markets will ultimately assure a fully employed economy that provides as much prosperity as its resources can produce. The basic axiomatic foundation of all these theories is the assumption that all market participants can "know" the economic future market outcomes from here to eternity[2] if not with perfect certainty, at least with knowledge of the objective probability risks involved and therefore with actuarial certainty. Accordingly all decision makers in these assumed "certain future" model can foresee any crisis coming and, in their own self interest, take any action necessary to avoid such a crisis from harming their own self-interest. Thus the classical system basic "known future" assumption led Greenspan to state in his congressional testimony, this classical theory told him that the function of managers of lending institutions would know the "self-interest of lending institutions to protect shareholders' equity" and therefore these managers would prevent their lending intuitions from taking the mistaken purchasing and holding securities action in the mortgage backed derivatives market. The theory indicated it was the function of the managers to "know" that at a specific future date the defaults of the subprime portion of the derivative securities will result in the market price collapse which destroyed much of the equity of shareholders. If the managers knew the future they would protect equity by selling these securities before the price collapse.

The Keynes–Post Keynesian liquidity theory of a market oriented economy, on the other hand, presumes business managers make important production decisions while realizing they do not know with certainty what is going to happen in the future. The fundamental assumption basis of Keynes' theory is (1) time is a device that prevents everything from happening at once, so that decisions made today will have their pay-out result at some future date days, weeks, months or even years in the future and (2) the economic future is uncertain and not readily predictable. Clearly there is a major difference between the classical view of a known predictable future and the Keynes' assumption that the economic future is uncertain and cannot be reliably predicted today.

In the Keynes theory, managers have to make decisions today regarding the level of production, employment, pricing, etc. without knowing for certain what the future results will be of these decisions. Accordingly, the development of legal forward money contracts for market transactions commits both parties to a contractual action at a specific future date The buyer on the contract can meet his/her commitment by the payment of a contractual specified sum of money. The seller can produce the item being sold at the specified contract date, or, if for any reason, the seller cannot deliver the item, he/she can meet this contractual commitment by paying the buyer a sum of money sufficient to cover the costs that the buyer experiences when the delivery is not made. Accordingly, the possession of liquidity, i.e., the ability to meet all legal money contractual obligations becomes an important aspect of all economic actions of all decision makers in the market economy.

The government has the duty to ensure enforcement of all these legal money contractual obligations. This permits decision makers to be relatively certain about contractual cash inflows and outflows over the otherwise uncertain future.

Thus, in the world in which we live, the government provides the institutions of money and money contracting *for all market transactions* whether they be for immediate (spot) transaction or for a forward specific transaction at a future date. *The sanctity of the money contract is the essence of the capitalist economic system* and the basic axiom of the Keynes theory.

All variants of classical theory, on the other hand, ignore money contracts by presuming all market transactions are made in terms of "real contracts" where, in essence, goods trade for goods between the transactors—as it would be in a barter economy. In other words, the classical explanation presumes the economy operates "as if" it is a barter economy.

Moreover since classical theory assumes that all decision makers can know the future, it follows that when a "real contract" is made in a free market system, both self-interested parties to the real contract "know" they will have the necessary real resources to meet their real contractual commitment. There can never be an honest market default in the theoretical classical system. Hence there is no need for government interference in the market place.

The conclusion of the Keynes–Post Keynesian system, however, is that the government, as the developer and enforcer of the money contracting system, can cure, with the cooperation of private industry and households, some major economic flaws that can occur in the operation of a capitalist market-oriented, money using economy when, in the absence of government action, unfettered greed and/or fear is permitted to dominate economic market transaction decisions.

Keynes produced a theory that would explain why there could be massive unemployment even in a competitive market economy that possesses perfectly flexible wages and prices but also uses money contracts for all market transactions. Accordingly, liquidity can be an important factor in making market decisions.

As Keynes stated:

"The classical theorists resemble Euclidean geometers in a non-Euclidean world who, discovering that in experience straight lines apparently parallel often meet, rebuke the lines for not keeping straight -as the only remedy for the unfortunate collisions which are occurring. Yet, in truth, there is no remedy except to overthrow the axiom of parallels and to work out a non-Euclidean geometry. Something similar is required today in economics."[3]

By overthrowing restrictive classical axioms Keynes developed a general theory that was equivalent to his call for a non-Euclidean type of economic theory. Keynes argued these classical axioms are not applicable to the monetary economy in which we live where entrepreneurs organize the production process by hiring workers to produce goods and services to be profitably sold for money in the market place.

The collision of apparent straight lines in a non-Euclidean world was the equivalent of classical economists observing massive unemployment in their world while their theory suggested that the competitive market economy should provide full employment for all who want to work. To the extent these classical theory economists observed the existence of unemployment, they explained that the unemployed workers were at fault for not being willing to accept a job at a lower market wage—a wage where all could be fully employed. In other words, the victims (unemployed workers) were blamed for their unemployment!

Keynes suggested that it was not the refusal of workers to accept a lower wage for getting employment that was the problem. Classical economic theory which professes that if workers would only accept lower wages all who wanted to work would be employed was not applicable to our economic system. Keynes argued that classical theory was a theory whose "teaching is misleading and disastrous if we attempt to apply it to the facts of experience".[4]

Unfortunately even in our time many so-called experts in economics—including Nobel Prize winners—continue to develop sophisticated models that still possess the fundamental axioms of classical economic theory that Keynes argued had to be discarded. Since these classical axioms lie below a mountain of mathematical and statistical computer analysis, they are difficult for the average person or even many trained economists to recognize. Nevertheless, the result of using these very technical classical axiomatic models have encouraged decisions by policy makers and regulators that are often misleading and disastrous—as Alan Greenspan admitted in his Congressional testimony.

Notes

1. I must admit that sometimes such changes of the facts happen in academia. For example Milton Friedman changed the definition of savings in his Permanent Income Theory to get the redefined facts to support his classical analysis. Keynes and most people would define savings as that portion of current income that is not used to purchase any producible goods. Friedman defines savings out of current income as equal to the purchase price of a newly produced durable goods, e.g., a new automobile. Since the automobile was expected to last for years, only the depreciation of the automobile in the current period is defined as consumption. The rest of the purchase price is defined as savings, where the utility (usefulness) of the auto was saved to be consumed as depreciation in each future period over the auto's useful life.
2. Nobel Prize winner Paul Samuelson wrote a book entitled *Foundatons of Economic Analysis (1947) Harvard University Press* which insists that any valid economic theory must have "Walrasin microfoundations" so that every decision maker in the system knows the market prices of everything not only today but for every day in the future.
3. *Op. cit.*, p. 16.
4. *Op. cit.*, p. 3.

3

Understanding the Role of Money and Money Contracts in a Market Economy

John Maynard Keynes wrote "...the ideas of economists and political philosophers, both when they are right and when they are wrong, are more powerful than is commonly understood. Indeed the world is ruled by little else".[1]

The ideas embodied in the classical economic theory continues to dominate the teaching o economics in academia as well as the economic policy decisions of government officials and central bankers. This is true despite Alan Greenspan's admission that he does not know why the classical economic theory, which won a Nobel Prize, failed to explain why managers of financial assets did not take actions to avoid the global financial crisis of 2007–2008.

Classical economic theory, though wrong, still is the power that dominates policy makers view of the operation of the economic system in which we live. Consequently economic policies in developed economies have not generated a rapidly economic recovery from the global financial crisis. Instead we are living in what is often called the "Great Recession" where the economy exhibits relatively low rates of growth, if it grows at all.

In this chapter we will examine the presumptive foundation of classical economic theory's ideas and their subsequent application to our economic world. We will indicate why these basic presumptions conflict with a most obvious important fact of our economic system, namely that it is essential to recognize the role of money and money contracts if we are to understand the operation of our market oriented economy.

Classical theory denies the fact that money and money denominated contracts play an important role in determining employment and the total production of the economy. This basic belief of classical theory has encouraged the adoption of economic policies that not only fail to resolve our economic problems, but often can worsen the economic distress of nations.

The fundamental conclusion of classical theory is that free competitive markets are perfect. At the micro level it is assumed that every participant in every market is all knowing not only with regard to market economic conditions today, but also each are all wise about what the economic conditions in every market will be for every day the future. Accordingly, in such a world where everyone supposedly knows the economic future, the self-interest of market participants allows each to make optimum decisions regarding what they must do to maximize and protect their income and wealth over time. That is why Alan Greenspan said that "those of us who had looked to the self interest of lending institutions to protect shareholders' equity (myself especially) are in a state of shocked disbelief...." The 2007–2008 global financial crisis showed that "the self interest of lending institutions" did not induce managers to take the necessary steps to protect "shareholders equity". Why?

Obviously either the managers of these institutions did not know what the "self interest" required, or, more likely, prior to 2007 the managers did not know what would happen in the future in financial markets and therefore, could not foresee the global financial markets crisis that started in 2007.

Greenspan's reliance on the evolving "vast risk management and pricing system ...[that combined] the best insights of mathematicians and finance experts supported by major advances in computer and communications technology" was bound to fail if in the real world of experience market participants faced an uncertain, not predictable financial future. The Nobel Prize that was awarded "for the discovery of the [free market] pricing model that underpins much of the advance in [financial] derivatives markets" requires the presumption that the economic future is known to market participants so they can take actions that protect their own self-interests and not become victims of the financial crisis. When it became obvious that the economic future is uncertain and therefore the global financial crisis was not foreseen by self-interested market participants, then, as Greenspan noted, the modern risk management theory edifice "collapsed" even though it was built by classical economists including a Nobel Prize winner.

If modern risk management theorists had understood the general theory analysis developed by Keynes, then they would have recognized that the role of money and money contracts is to provide a handle for market participants to deal with the fact that the economic future is uncertain.

Just think, dear reader, what optimal decisions you could make to buy or sell specific stocks on the stock market if you know not only the price of the stocks today but also the price of the same stock tomorrow, next week, month, etc. Is there any doubt you, and every other decision maker in the stock market, would be free to make decisions that would maximize your income and wealth without any help, or intervention by the government? Would you get caught holding derivative securities whose market value was about to collapse, if you could foresee the financial market price collapse coming?

It should be recognized that classical theory assumes that in a market where participants know the economic future and are free to make any decision they desire, the resulting market activity will successfully solve every person's economic problems that may arise even if the system is subject to an economic shock.

Let us illustrate how this all knowing approach explains that in a free market, full employment will always occur. If, at any point of time, there should be unemployed workers, that is the supply of workers wanting to work exceeded the employers' demand to hire workers at the going money wage rate, then in a free market, the wage would instantaneously decline. The classical theory then presumes that this market wage decline would offer entrepreneurs in every industry more profit opportunities as the labor costs of production would be reduced while it is assumed market demand remained unchanged. The lower labor cost would permit firms to sell more products at a lower price and still make more profits. If entrepreneurs can sell more product profitably, then it is in their self interest to hire more workers as the market wage rate declines. Consequently, classical theory insists that at some lower market money wage all workers who wanted to work at that reduced market wage would be employed, while profit seeking entrepreneurs would "know" that when they hired more workers at a lower wage to produce additional output, there would still be sufficient future market demand so that all the additional output would be profitably sold!

In other words, it is an unproven presumption of classical theory that at some [lower] money wage, there always will be sufficient market demand for all the products of industry to sold at a future market price that assures entrepreneurs they will make more profits by hiring the unemployed. This classical theory presumption that entrepreneurs can know future labor market conditions as well as future market demand for their products. implies that significant unemployment of labor occurs only because workers refuse to accept lower wages. This refusal to accept lower wage may be because labor unions insist on some standardized union wage and/or governments put a floor under the legal minimum wage—where this floor is higher than the free market wage that assures full employment. Thus, in classical theory, it is truculent workers insisting on some rigid wage floor that is the basic cause of observed unemployment.

In this classical theory unemployment could persist only if workers refused to accept the lower money wage that assured full employment. Union tend to prevent workers from accepting wage reductions. Minimum wage legislation also can prevent workers from accepting lower market wages. The result will be that any rigidity or stickiness in money wages that prevents wages from falling can prevent the market from providing full employment with profitable sales of products and prosperous workers. In this classical explanation of the operation of our market oriented economic system, the villains that prevent the markets from assuring a persistent full employment economy are unions, minimum wage laws, and workers' truculence to accept lower money wages. The unemployed workers are not innocent victims, they are the villains that caused their unemployed status and inability to earn income.

Winston Churchill once said "No one pretends that democracy is perfect or all-wise. Indeed, it has been said that democracy is the worst form of government except for all those other forms that have been tried from time to time". Keynes's theory of the operation of our market oriented, money-using economy is that our economic system can be characterized as similar to Churchill's description of democracy. Keynes's theory suggests that no one should pretend that participants in market-oriented, money using capitalist system are perfect or all-wise and consequently government should never interfere with free markets. We should recognize a free market system may have some serious economic flaws Nevertheless, despite these faults, our market oriented capitalist system is better than any other form of economic system that have been tried historically.

What are these flaws in our economic system? If the cause of these faults can be identified then, Keynes believed that human ingenuity can develop policies that eliminate, or at least mitigate, these faults.

Keynes wrote that "The outstanding faults of the economic society in which we live are its failure to provide full employment and its arbitrary and inequitable distribution of income and wealth".[2] Keynes's analysis demonstrated that it is not the rigidity of market wages that causes significant unemployment and large inequalities of income and wealth in the normal operations of our market oriented, money using system. Once the Keynes theory identified the true causes of such faults in our economic system then the theory can suggest policies that can solve, or at least reduce the severity of, these major flaws of a capitalist economy. That is what the theory that Keynes developed to replace classical economic theory can do. And that is why no one should fear the policies advocated by John Maynard Keynes.

The Classical Presumptions That Keynes Overthrew

Let us specifically examine the classical theory's fundamental axioms that Keynes claimed prevented classical theory from providing a useful explanation of the operation of our market-oriented economic system. Keynes argued that just as mathematicians have recognized that the parallel axiom is not applicable to non-Euclidean geometry, so should economists recognize that there are basic classical axioms that are not applicable to the operation of our money using economic system. If economists overthrow the inapplicable presumptive foundations of classical economic theory, then economists can provide a more relevant explanation for understanding of the operation of our market economy, its flaws, and how we can develop policies to improve the operation of the system.

The basic false presumption of classical economic theory is the assumption that we have already identified, namely the assertion that evert participant in each market are all wise and can know the future, i.e., the economic future can be accurately predicted.

Time is a device that prevents all things from happening at once. An economic decision made at any moment in time will have its outcome (pay out) minutes, hours, days, weeks, months, or even years in the future. Given all possible alternative actions that one can choose in the market place at any moment in time, how can any self-interested decision maker choose the specific alternative action that will provide him/her with the greatest income or pleasure in the forthcoming future? Only if the decision maker knows precisely what the future (payout) outcome of all possible alternative decisions will be, can the choice made always be the optimum decision.

Classical theory presumes self-interested decision makers are all wise and therefore already "know" precisely what will the pay-off in the future be as a result of any specific decision that they can make today. The result is that if all persons are free to make market decisions that they "know" will be in their best self-interest, then all the economy's resources will be efficiently allocated towards the processes of production and exchange which yield the highest possible returns in the known future of markets for every inhabitant of our economic system. In other words, when the future is known to all self-interested decision makers, then markets are assumed to be efficient in the sense they produce things that are most beneficial to all participants in the market. Government interference in the market place can only make things worse! It is this presumed efficiency of all financial markets that led Alan Greenspan to believe, before 2007, that the deregulation of financial markets would prevent any global financial crisis from happening.

In the 19th century classical economic theory merely assumed that all individuals "knew" the future with perfect certainty. In the late 19th century, a French economist Leon Walras set out a mathematical deterministic system of equations as the most extensive description of the old classical theory of decision makers knowing the economic future with perfect certainty. In this Walrasian system, at any point in time, spot markets exist for people to enter into "real" contracts for transactions to buy and/or sell things or services today as well as forward markets exists for people to enter into real contracts for transactions to buy and sell things or services for every possible future date. Walras assumed there exists today a market auctioneer for every one of these spot and forward markets. The auctioneer provided every potential market participant today with complete information about every market price and outcome for all spot markets and all forward markets for every day from here to eternity. Thus, by assumption, each market participant in the Walrasian system always knew the price and output for every possible product for ever possible date from here to eternity.

In the 20th century Nobel Laureate Kenneth Arrow and Gerard Debreu formulated an even more general version of this mathematical Walrasian system where in addition to spot and forward markets for all goods and services there was incorporated a complete set of contingency (insurance) markets. Accordingly all market transactions one makes could be insured against all possible accidental damaging contingencies at any future date. So not only would all decision makers "know" the economic future but they could insure themselves against any accidental factor that might otherwise damage their choice. Believe it or not this generalized mathematical formulation underlies all modern classical economic theory today including the "Keynesians" sub classical theories!

Ultimately this type of classical analysis to explain why all market participants know the future led to the theory of "rational expectations" developed by Nobel Laureate Robert Lucas of the University of Chicago. Lucas attempted to use modern probability theory (technically known as stochastic theory) to explain how people in the market through their "rational expectations" about the future would actually "know" the probability of every possible future outcome at any future date.

In this rational expectations analysis all future outcomes are presumed to be govern by an objective probability distribution.[3] The only question becomes how do decision makers today form their expectations about the objective probability distributions that govern all future outcomes so they can know the future.

Lucas postulated that if self-interested individuals are "rational" humans, then their expectations must be "rational" in the sense that these expectations provide correct information about the probabilities that will govern all outcomes in the future. If these expectations were not rational, then these humans could not make rational decisions that maximize their income and wealth. In Lucas's terminology the subjective probability distribution that existed today in any "rational" decision maker's mind about any future date market outcomes is assumed to be equal to the true objective probability distribution that actually will govern that future date's market outcomes.

How can people obtain information today to form these rational (assumed correct) expectations about all future probabilities associated with any given future date? Statisticians tell you that if characteristics (descriptions) about any event or outcome are governed by a probability process, then knowledge about these characteristics can be obtained. All that is required to make statistically reliable probability forecasts about the characteristics of any specific dated outcomes is for the analyst to draw a sample from the type of events occurring at those future dates and statistically analyze the sample data obtained.

Since drawing a sample from events occurring in the future is impossible to obtain today, rational expectations theorists presume that the probability distribution that governed past and current economic outcomes will be the same as the probability distribution that governs all future outcomes. Thus, if an analyst feeds enough past and current economic statistics into a computer, then the analyst can get the computer to convert all this data into a probability distribution of possible outcomes. The result, it is presumed, will be a reliable statistical model that allows the model user to correctly predict the future as long as the past probability distribution is the same as the one that governs the future outcomes.

The reader should recognize that many international agencies such as the International Monetary Fund, as well as national central banks such as the Federal Reserve and other government agencies such as the United States President's Council of Economic Advisers, as well as private companies have built such statistical models that presume past data will permit them to predict the future. Yet, none of these many statistical models apparently predicted the global financial crisis of 2007–2008.

One of the leaders of this rational expectations school of economic theory and a Nobel Prize winner, Thomas Sargent, has suggested the problem with relying on this rational expectations economic theory model is that it can describe an economic world that may be very different from our world of experience. Sargent has written that the rational expectations theory "imputes to the people inside the model much *more knowledge about* the system they are operating in than is available to the economist or econometrician who is using the model to try to understand their behavior. In particular, an econometrician faces the problem of *estimating* probability distributions and laws of motion that the agents in the model are assumed to know".[4]

But if Sargent is correct regarding a model that he received a Nobel Prize for helping to develop, then it should be readily understood that the statistical models used by government agencies presume that people in our markets have "much *more knowledge abou*t the system they are operating in than is available to the economist or econometrician" hired by government to help politicians create legislative regulations and policies to affect the economy.

Under this classical theory model of how rational decision makers behave, it is clear that all government policies that regulate or interfere with market activities can not improve the optimal outcome that the classical theory presumes will occur if rational decision makers know the future and are free to make their own decisions regarding their actions.

As an illustration of what this implies, let us examine the science of astronomy which utilizes this probability approach as a foundation of its theory of to explain the future movement of heavenly bodies. The theory of astronomy accepted by all astronomers is that since the moment of the "Big Bang" creation of the universe, the future paths of all the heavenly bodies are predetermined by natural immutable laws that cannot be changed by any human action. By using past data measurements of velocity and direction of heavenly bodies, astronomers can predict accurately, within a few seconds, when and where the next solar eclipse will be visible on earth. Congress, or a Parliament, cannot pass an enforceable law to eliminate the next solar eclipse in order to increase the amount of sunshine the earth receives so as to increase total agricultural production and thereby improve the availability of food in the economy and thereby increase the gross domestic product (GDP) of the economy.

Similarly, if this presumption of the movement of the economy in the future can be determined by statistical analysis of past markets movements, then just as the government cannot legislate changes in solar eclipses, government policies will not be able to legislate improvements in economic movement outcomes already predetermined by the objective probability distributions governing past and future events. Accepting the assumption of a predetermined optimal probabilistic future implies the economic philosophy of *laissez-faire* i.e., government should never interfere in markets since it cannot change the long run path of the economy any more than legislation can change the paths of the moon and the earth around the sun in order to prevent future solar eclipses from occurring.

If one accepts the classical assumption that today's decision makers can know, or at least obtain probabilities by statistical analysis of past data, then the future path of our market economy can be obtained by analyzing samples from the past. This information will permit people to make the correct decisions in the market to maximize the welfare of everyone in the community. Consequently classical theory declares that the market is efficient in the use of resources of the economy. The government should not interfere in the market place.

Lawrence Summers, former Secretary of the Treasury and economic adviser to President Obama has stated that "the ultimate social functions [of efficient financial markets] are spreading risks, guiding the investment of scarce capital, and processing and disseminating the information [about the future] possessed by diverse traders.... prices will always reflect fundamental values.... The logic of efficient markets is compelling".[5]

The logic of the efficient market theory is compelling only *if* one accepts the presumption of classical theory that the future is known and not uncertain. For financial markets to be efficient under the Summers' vision, information about the future exists, and market participants must know, either with certainty or at least via probabilistic statistical reliability, future revenues and profits that will be associated with the enterprises underlying the securities being traded in the financial markets. These presumed to be known future revenues associated with the enterprise's use of productive capital are captured in what Summers calls today's "fundamentals". If financial markets are so efficient, then how does one explain that the financial markets for mortgage backed derivatives after operating supposedly efficiently for several years suddenly collapsed in 2007 and thereby brought about the financial market crisis of 2007–2008? As Alan Greenspan found out it is difficult to explain why there was a global financial crisis if markets are efficient, as classical Nobel Prize winning theories claim. In later chapters, when we lay out Keynes's theory of the importance of liquidity in our economic system, we will be able to explain why the possibility of a financial market collapse can occur when the economic future is uncertain and therefore when financial market collapse will occur cannot be accurately predicted.

Keynes criticized classical theory where "fact and expectations were assumed to be given in a definite form and risks ...were supposed to be capable of an exact actuarial computation. The calculus of probability... was supposed capable of reducing uncertainty to the same calculable state as that of certainty itself....I accuse the classical economic theory of being itself one of those pretty, polite techniques which tries to deal with the present by abstracting from the fact we know very little about the future....[Every classical economist] has overlooked the precise nature of the difference his abstraction makes between theory and practice and the character of the fallacies which he is likely to be led".[6]

Keynes argued that "the fact [is] that our knowledge of the future is fluctuating, vague, and uncertain,.... By 'uncertain' I do not mean merely to distinguish what is known for certain from what is only probable. The game of roulette is not subject, in this sense, to uncertainty.... About these [future economic outcomes] matters there is no scientific basis on which to form any calculable probability".[7]

According to Keynes probabilities calculated from samples drawn from the economic past should not be viewed as actuarial information about future events. Or as Nobel Prize winner Sir John Hicks wrote "One must assume that people in one's model [theory] do not know what is going to happen, and know that they do not know what is going to happen. As in history".[8]

Keynes believed that intelligent action by government could reduce, if not completely eliminate, the major faults of the capitalist, market oriented economy in which we live. Accordingly, Keynes had to overthrow the classical presumption that the future can be known by today's market participants. In a theory where the future is uncertain, *laissez faire* is not an applicable philosophy. There can be a role for government to play to help avoid economic distress.

Unfortunately, all mainstream economic theorists, whether they label themselves Classical Theorists, Monetarists, Efficient Market theorists, Old Neoclassical Synthesis Keynesians or even New Keynesians still require their theories to be based on the Walrasian micro-presumption that market participants are knowledgable and all-wise .about the future. The aforementioned economists who still call themselves "Keynesians" (e.g. Nobel Laureates, Paul Samuelson, Robert Solow, Paul Krugman, Joseph Stiglitz) still have a basic assumption that the future is at least knowable to market participants as a foundation in their Old and New Keynesian theories. Nevertheless these "Keynesians" advocate government policy actions rather than inaction. They justify their recommendation of government taking immediate policy actions on the basis that (1) in the short run wages and prices are not sufficiently flexible and therefore it takes too long for a Walrasian type classical system to readjust after a shock that causes unemployment; or (2) there is asymmetric information existing today so that some market participants know the future but others are fools who are not smart enough to know how to obtain the correct information about the future objective probability distributions from data that exists today. These fools keep making wrong decisions in the market. These wrong decisions can cause recessions and depressions.

In essence these self proclaimed "Keynesians", really are classical theorists who are impatient with the time they believe it takes the free market to reestablish a full employment position when some shock shakes the economy temporarily. They want government action immediately. As we will see in forthcoming chapters, these "Keynesians" apparently never understood the general theory that Keynes developed. Accordingly it was left to the Post Keynesian economists to revive Keynes's actual theory and develop its contents to be applicable for our market-oriented, money using entrepreneurial economy.

A Second False Classical Assumption

The classical belief that the future can be known to all market participants implies that the future path of total production and employment is predetermined and ultimately immutable—just as the future path of heavenly bodies is in astronomy is predetermined and cannot be changed by human action. Accordingly, if tomorrow's total output and employment (and thus total real income of the economy) is already predetermined, then classical theory has no role for money to play in determining future output and employment. The classical analysis requires an additional assumption known as the neutral money axiom. This neural money presumes that in any future calendar time period, any additional increase in the quantity of money supplied to the economy will have no effect on causing changes in the (predetermined) total output produced (GDP) or employment in that future period. This neutral money assumption is the basis of what economists call the Quantity Theory of Money.

Milton Friedman, the Nobel Prize Laureate is closely associated with this Quantity Theory of Money, where changes in the quantity of money directly affect changes in the price level. Thus, Friedman argues that if the predetermined increase in total output in the economy is 3% in any future year, then that year's supply of money created by the central bank (such as the Federal Reserve) should increase by only 3% to avoid inflation and keep the price level constant. If the money supply increases by more than the predetermined future 3% rise in total real output, then inflation is inevitable.

Friedman has described his belief in the neutral money assumption as follows:

> "We have accepted the quantity theory presumption… that changes in the quantity of money as such *in the long run* have a negligible effect on real income, so that nonmonetary forces are 'all that matter' for changes in real income [total production or GDP] over the decades and 'money does not matter'. On the other hand, we have regarded the quantity of money, … as all that matter for…. the price level."[9]

Oliver Blanchard, who is the economics advisor to the International Monetary Fund and was also a professor at the Massachusetts Institute of Technology's and a research economist at the prestigious National Bureau of Economic Research, has characterized all the mainstream economic theory models widely used by economists at government agencies, central banks, in academia, etc. as follows :

> "All the models we have seen impose the neutrality of money as a maintained assumption. This is very much a matter of faith, based on theoretical considerations rather than on empirical evidence."[10]

If the growth of real output of goods and services produced in any future period is a predetermined knowable, then if the government (or the central bank) increases the money supply that can be spent on produced goods and services by a greater growth rate, then the only effect in classical theory will be that of inflation, i.e., the price of the predetermined level of produced goods and services will rise. Or as Milton

Friedman was fond of saying "Inflation occurs when too much money is chasing too few goods".

Accordingly Friedman's belief that real output has a long term tendency to grow at 3% per annum results in Friedman advocating a monetary policy of a 3% rule for money supply growth rather than leaving it to the discretion of central bankers as to how much of a change n the money supply should occur in any period. Given the neutral money presumption, the central bank use of its monetary policy can only directly affect the rate of inflation in the economy.

To ease the problems created by the global financial crisis, the Federal Reserve began its "Quantitative Easing" or QE policy of creating money by buying huge quantities of government bonds and mortgage backed derivative securities. This QE policy immediately brought a reaction from many economists who still presumed the neutral money assumption in their analysis. These media "experts" predicted that the QE policy will create a significant increase in the price level, or even runaway inflation. In the period from 2009 to 2014, the Federal Reserve QE policy almost quadrupled the amount of reserves that banks have on deposit with Federal Reserve resulting in a potential huge increase in the money supply.

What has been the inflationary effect of QE? An article in the *Wall Street Journal* of January 29, 2009 written by J. Hilsenrath and L. Rappaport indicated that this QE policy "some might see it…as an inflationary move to finance deficits by printing money". Yet after more than eight years later, despite the huge increase in the quantity of money stimulated by the Fed's QE policy, the rate of inflation in the US in 2017 is less than the 2% per annum rate the Fed see as a necessary inflationary price target if the economy is to perform strongly.

Keynes believed that money is never neutral and that changes in the quantity of money can affect the level of output and employment. He wrote:

> "An economy which uses money but uses it merely as a *neutral* link between transactions in real things and real assets and does not allow it to enter into motives or decisions, might be called - for want of a better name - a real exchange economy. The theory which I desiderate would

deal, in contradistinction to this, with an economy in which money plays a part on its own and affects motives and decisions and is, in short, one of the operative factors in the situation, so that the course of events cannot be predicted either in the long period or in the short, without a knowledge of the behavior of money between the first state and the last. And it is this which we ought to mean when we speak of a *monetary economy*. … Booms and depressions are peculiar to an economy in which money is not neutral. I believe that the next task is to work out in some detail such a monetary theory of production. That is a the task on which I am now occupying myself in some confidence that I am not wasting my time".[11]

In essence, the neutral money, *real exchange* economy is equivalent to a barter economy where money has no role to play in determining output and employment. Accordingly all classical theories are based on Walrasian analysis that presumes the future is known and money is neutral are basically descriptions of a barter economy, and not a money using economic system. Once the neutrality of money and a future that is knowable presumptions are rejected as theory foundations, then an organizing principle for studying the level of employment and output in a market economy involves (1) comprehending the role of money as a means of settling contractual obligations and (2) understanding the essential role liquidity plays in determining the flow of production and employment in the economic system in which we live.

James K. Galbraith has noted that the first three words of the title of Keynes's 1936 book *The General Theory of Employment, Interest and Money* "are evidently cribbed from Albert Einstein".[12] Einstein's general theory of relativity had displaced Newton's classical theory in physics that had maintained the separation of time and space. Einstein's demonstrated that the time-space continuum is, in essence the extension of non-Euclidean geometry of curved spaces. Keynes hoped to mimic Einstein's revolutionary general theory of relativity and displace the classical economic theory that maintained the separation of market outcomes and the money supply implied by the neutral money presumption. Keynes wanted to replace this assumed market from money separation with the equivalent of a market-money curved space continuum, i.e., where money and market outcomes continuously interact.

To accept Keynes's logic and its Post Keynesian development, however, threatens the Panglossian conclusion that, in the long run, all is for the best in this best of all possible worlds where a market economy free of all government regulations and interference assures full employment and prosperity for all those who want to work. Throwing over the classical presumption that the future is knowable and money is neutral permitted Keynes to produce his more general theory that allows for the possibility that an entrepreneurial system might possess some inherent faults such as its failure to provide for full employment even in the long run. Keynes's logic is just as antithetical to the Social Darwinist classical economic theory as the view on the origin of human life as asserted by the "scientific theory of evolution" is to the "intelligent design" view of some fundamentalist Christian religious belief in the literal biblical explanation of the creation of life in the story of Adam and Eve and the Garden of Eden.

Keynes's general theory suggests that this inability of the entrepreneurial market oriented system to provide full employment can be ameliorated by developing corrective fiscal policies to assure sufficient market demand and regulatory institutions for stabilizing our financial markets and not relying solely on monetary policies as "the only game in town". There can be a permanent role for government to correct systemic economic faults of the entrepreneurial system in which we live while preserving the freedom of entrepreneurial decision making and innovation.

The Third False Classical Presumption

Classical theory assumes that anything sold in any market must be a gross substitute for anything else for sale in a market. This gross substitution assumption means that a decline in the relative market price of any specific good or service will induce buyers to buy more of the item that is now cheaper and less of the items that have become relatively more expensive while spending the same total amount of income. For example, if tea and coffee are gross substitutes then if the price of tea increases, people will buy less tea and purchase more coffee.

In a later chapter we will explain how Keynes's theory rejected the gross substitution axiom as applicable to the things that savers use to store their savings out of current income. An act of saving means that a saver is not spending his/her entire income currently on the purchase of producible goods and services. Instead savers attempt to use their savings out of money income to purchase some durable thing that they can carry into the indefinite future (with minimum carrying cost) until a time comes when they wish to spend these savings on producibles.

We will see that in Keynes's theory of a money using economy, savers always store their savings in durables such as money and/or other liquid financial assets. Savers never store their savings in producible goods. In other words, readily producible goods are not good substitutes for liquid assets as a form for carrying one's savings into the uncertain future. When Keynes described the process of people saving out of current income in a money using economy, he assumed that for storing savings over time, producible durable goods were not a gross substitute for liquid assets such as tradable financial assets and currency and money bank balances.[13] The mere act of savings threatens full employment outcomes since a penny saved is a penny not spent on producibles and thereby cannot be income earned by somebody contributing to the production of a good or service.

Notes

1. J. M. Keynes, *The General theory of employment, interest and Money*, p. 383
2. *Op cit.*, p. 372.
3. The term "objective" for the probability distribution is used to suggest it is created by natural parameters and cannot be altered by anything people decide to do today.
4. T. Sargent, *Bounded Rationality in Macroeconomics*, (Clarendon Press, Oxford, 1993, p. 21.
5. L. H. Summers and V. P. Summers, "When Financial Markets Work Too Well: A Cautious Case for a Securities Transaction Tax", *Journal of Financial Services, 3*, (1989), p. 166.
6. J. M. Keynes, Letter of 4 July 1938 to R. F. Harrod reprinted in *The Collected Writings of John Maynard Keynes, 14*, edited by D. Moggridge (Macmillan, London, 1963) pp.112–115.

7. J. M. Keynes, "The General Theory of Employment", *Quarterly Journal of Economics (1937)*, reprinted in *The Collected Writings of John Maynard Keynes, vol xiv,* pp. 113–114. edited by D. Moggridge (Macmillan, :London, 1973).
8. J. R. Hicks, *Economic Perspectives* (Oxford, Oxford Economic Press, 1977) p. vii.
9. M. Friedman, "A Theoretical Framework for Monetary analysis", in *Milton Friedman's Monetary Framework* edited by T. J. Gordon, (university of Chicago Press, Chicago, 1970) p. 27
10. O. Blanchard, "Why Does Money Affect Output?", in *Handbook of Monetary Economics, 2*, edited by B. M. Friedman and F. H. Hahn, (North Holland, New York, 1990), p. 828.
11. J. M. Keynes, "A Monetary Theory of Production", reprinted in *The Collected Writings of John Maynard Keynes, 13*, edited by D. Moggridge (Macmillan, London, 1973), pp. 408–411.
12. J. K. Galbraith, "Keynes, Einstein, and the Scientific Revolution" in *Keynes, Money and the Open Economy* edited by P. Arestis (Elgar, Cheltenham, 1996) p. 14.

4

Unemployment: Why Can't People Who Want to Work Find Jobs?

The income principle behind Keynes's theory is simple. Income is earned whenever a newly produced good or service is sold in the market place. For example, when a person spends money to buy this book new, the total purchase price (or cost) of this book contributes to the income of the book seller, who, in turn, has paid part of this purchase price to contribute to the income of the publisher who uses part to pay income to its employees. The publisher also has paid a sum to the income of the printer for printing the book. Furthermore, the publisher contributes to the author's income by making a royalty payment equal to a contractual agreed upon percentage of the monetary funds received from the book seller. Any remaining sum of the money sum received by the publisher is the profit income of the publishing firm.

The important principle involved here is that whatever is the purchase cost to a buyer of a newly produced good or service becomes income to the people and firms that has produced and sold the item purchased. In other words, every dollar of income people spend out of current income on newly produced items, becomes a dollar of income for someone else in the economy.

In general we look to private enterprise to produce most of the products that generate most of the jobs in our economy. In order for workers and business enterprises to earn income they must engage in the production of goods and services that someone willingly buys in the market place. It therefore follows that managers of business firms will employ more workers as long as these managers expect to sell all the output produced by the workers at a profitable price in the market.

Unemployment occurs when managers do not expect sufficient market demand to be able to profitably sell the additional output that the unemployed workers, if hired, could have helped to produce. Consequently, the basic cause of unemployment in the economy is a lack of sufficient profitable market demand to encourage private sector entrepreneurs to hire all the workers who are willing to work at the going market wage.

Of course not all production and employment occurs in the private sector of the economy. Some productions and employment involve hiring by government to provide services directly to the public, e.g., police, fire, and military protection; while some government services may actually be sold to the public, e.g., postal service, the use of toll bridges and roads. In general, however, in our market oriented economic system we expect most jobs to be created by private sector firms hiring workers to produce products that can be profitably sold in the market.

Consequently, in situations of recession and/or depression when unemployment is a significant economic problem, any government policy designed to reduce unemployment and move the system towards a more prosperous full employment economy must be a policy that helps to generate additional market demand spending for the goods and services that are produced by domestic industries.

Suppose a household decides not to spend all its current income on goods and services and instead decides to save some income for retirement years. When a household decides to save part of one's current income, then this household is deciding not to spend all of its income immediately on producible goods and services. Instead, in our economy, savings is used to purchase bonds and corporate stocks sold in financial markets or else merely kept as part of an unused bank account balance or even currency in a safe box at home. Any household savings out of current income, in effect, denies other people the ability to earn income that they would have earned if the household had decided not to save; but rather to spend all of their income on currently newly produced goods and services. In other words, a penny saved out of current income denies someone the ability to earn that penny as income.

In developing his general theory, it became obvious to Keynes that the classical conception of savings was not the conception of denying others the ability to earn income. Rather classical theorists considered savings as a rather vague notion that meant different things in different contexts.

In Keynes's time, the basic classical theory presumed that a decision to save was a decision to order to purchase, via a forward market, a specific producible good or service to be delivered at a specific date in the future. Savings was merely what classical theorists called a "time preference" ordering for each day in the future what goods to buy out of that part of today's income that households did not spend to buy goods and services today. Thus in classical theory all current income was always spent on producible goods and services as decision makers enter into what were called "real" contracts (not money) that involved the buying and selling of goods and services today and/or in the future. In essence this was a description of market transactions in a barter economy where goods always trade only for other goods. Under such a theory, saving for retirement would involve the household in using every dollar value of current "real" income "saved" today to forward contractually order what specific food, clothing, etc. they would want to be delivered to their home on specific days of retirement. For classical theorists savings merely was creating specific market demand for business managers to hire workers and create production schedules for today and the future.

Under the influence of the philosopher G. E. Moore,[1] Keynes recognized that a precise taxonomy regarding classification of spending and saving events in economics, like in biology, is crucial to scientific structure. As Keynes' first biographer, Roy Harrod noted: "The real defect with the classical system was that it deflected attention from what most needed attention. It was Keynes' extraordinary powerful intuitive sense of what was important that convinced him the old classification system was inadequate."[2]

Consequently, Keynes found it necessary to develop precise definition regarding different categories of spending out of current income in order to understand the cause of unemployment in the economic system. Keynes explanation of why there could be a lack of sufficient aggregate market demand for the goods and services that could be produced at full employment depended on providing a precise definition of savings out of current income—a definition that was different than what classical "time preference" savings theory required.

Keynes stated that all income earned by households could be classified into two categories—namely, consumption spending and savings. Keynes defined consumption spending as that portion of current income of households that is used to buy currently produced goods and services primarily from private sector business firms. Savings of households is then defined as that portion of current money income that is not used currently to buy producible goods and services. Or as Keynes put it "An act of individual savings means—so to speak—a decision not to have dinner to-day. But it does *not* necessitate a decision to have dinner or buy a pair of boots a week hence or a year hence or to consume any specified thing at any specified date. Thus it depresses the business of preparing to-day's dinner without stimulating the business of making ready for some future act of consumption."[3]

Keynes then noted that in a monetary economy savers had to store their savings in the form of some durable that could be held over a period of time with little or no carrying costs for the saver holding the durable over time. Accordingly as long as there were some durables such as liquid financial assets that possessed little or no carrying costs it became obvious that real durable goods such as plant, equipment, automobiles and other consumer durables would not be bought merely to store savings since the depreciation costs of holding such real assets over time would result in a significant loss in value if the durable was held as form of savings. Instead, Keynes defined savings out of current income as that portion of income that was held in the form of money (currency and bank deposits) and/or bonds, equity securities, or other financial liquid assets. Financial assets would be liquid if they can be readily bought with money and resold for money with little or no carrying costs or marketing costs (e.g., broker's fees) in a financial market.

Why are money and liquid assets so important as the things used to store current savings?

Keynes's theory of savings and liquidity involves developing a serious monetary theory for all domestic and international market transactions. This theory emphasizes that *all market transactions* involving production and exchanges in a modern, market oriented economy are organized via the use of legal money denominated contracts.

Why money contracts? Keynes' theory emphasizes the use of money contracts is an important way economic decision makers in the marketplace could deal with the problem of uncertainty about the future outcomes of today's decisions in our economic system. This legal money contracting view provides a new way of economic thinking to explain the operations of a monetary economy where entrepreneurs and households enter into money denominated contracts in order to help deal with the uncertain future.

We live in an economy with an irrevocable past and an uncertain future. In this world, decision makers know that they do not, and cannot, know with any degree of certainty the real economic future of producible goods, services, and employment. Yet they must live with decisions made today whose real outcome can only be known in the future. Accordingly, our economic system has developed the institution of legal money contracts that are used to organize *all* market production and exchange transactions. The use of money contracts provides buyer and seller decision makers with at least some legal contractual certainty and control over future cash inflows and outflows resulting from today's economic actions. Money contracts over time produce the concept of liquidity for individuals where possessing "liquidity" involves the ability to meet one's money contractual obligations as they come due. This liquidity concept is an essential aspect of market decision making in a capitalist economy with a financial market system. The need for liquidity affects all economic motives and decisions in the market place of such an economy.

The sanctity of money contracts is the essence of the capitalist system and of Keynes's analysis. Liquidity, i.e., the ability to meet one's money contractual commitments domestically and internationally becomes an essential foundation for understanding what affects motives and decisions to enter into market transaction contractual agreements in the operation of our entrepreneurial market oriented, money using economy.

Under the civil law of contracts, money is the thing that a government decides will settle all legal contractual obligations. Since the government not only makes and enforces the legal system, but the government also determines what is the thing called money that legally will settle all legal contractual obligations. All law abiding citizens find their need for liquidity typically takes the form of maintaining a positive balance in their bank deposit checkbook and currency in their wallets so all contractual obligations can be met as they come due. If, at any time, one's bank deposit is close to being overdrawn, the typical solution is either:

1. stop entering into additional money contractual payment obligations until more of one's cash inflow is received to increase one's deposit into one's bank account, or
2. arrange for a bank line of credit or
3. sell a liquid financial asset in one's portfolio and use the money to replenish one's bank account.

Since the future is uncertain, individual decision makers never know when they might suddenly be faced with a money contractual payment obligation at a future date that they did not, or could not, anticipate and/or that they cannot meet out of the cash inflows expected at that future date. Decision makers also never know if an expected cash inflow will suddenly disappear for any unexpected reason; e.g., a reduction in pension income due to financial market value declines, or a loss of job, or the death of the breadwinner in the family, or government austerity program that impacts the decision maker's cash inflow, or an asset that was held in one's portfolio that was thought to be liquid (i.e., could easily be sold for money)—such as mortgage backed derivatives—suddenly becomes illiquid and therefore cannot be readily sold for money.

Accordingly there is a precautionary liquidity motive for maintaining a positive bank deposit balance in order to protect against any unforeseen cash flow problems. *In our society, no one can either be too handsome, or too beautiful or too liquid.* As long as the future is uncertain, enhancing one's liquidity position will cushion the blow of any contractual obligations that may occur. The more one fears the economic uncertain future, the bigger liquidity security cushion is desirable. Savings out of current income are always stored in the form of money or other durable liquid assets that are not costly to hold and can be readily and inexpensively converted into money to meet any future contractual obligations.

Keynes wrote that money "comes into existence along with debts, which are contracts for deferred payments. And price lists, which are offers of contracts for sale or purchase...Money itself, [is] namely by delivery of which debt contracts and price contracts are *discharged* and in the shape of which a store of general purchasing power is held... Furthermore it is a peculiar characteristic of money contracts that it is the State or community not only which enforces delivery, but also which decides what it is that must be delivered as a lawful ...discharge of a contract... And the age of chartalist or State money was reached when the State claimed the right to declare what thing should answer as money... when it claimed the right not only to enforce the dictionary but also to write the dictionary. To-day all civilised money is, beyond the possibility of dispute, chartalist."[4]

What distinguishes the Keynes–Post Keynesian analysis from classical mainstream macroeconomic theory involves an analysis of whether decision makers can know with certainty the economic future involving real or money payouts and economic events. In classical theory analysis it is presumed decision makers know the future, or, at least, have rational expectations about the future that provide decision makers with actuarial certain correct knowledge about the future.

Keynes and his Post Keynesian followers[5] reject any classical assumption that presumes people can "know" the economic future. The rational for such a rejection is that the economic future is not predetermined. Rather the economic future it will be created by people's motivations, and liquidity behavior in the marketplace. Keynes and the Post Keynesians insist that people "know" they cannot know the future outcome of important and crucial economic decisions made today. The future is truly uncertain and not just probabilistic risky.

The Keynes alternative to the classical theory assumes an uncertain economic environment in terms of production of goods and services. Yet, it provides one with an understanding of the operation and functioning of financial markets in a capitalist system. The primary function of all well organized and orderly financial markets is to provide liquidity so that holders of financial assets traded on such orderly markets "know" they can make a *fast exit* from their liquid financial asset portfolio by selling their securities for money at a price close to the previous price in the market. For business firms and households the maintenance of one's liquid position to meet all possible future contractual obligations is of prime importance if illiquidity and possible bankruptcy are to be avoided. In our economic world, bankruptcy is the economic equivalent of a walk to the gallows.

Savings and Liquidity

Saving is the attempt of savers to put some of today's cash income inflow that is not spent to buy goods and services into some low carrying cost time-machine to carry the contractual settlement (purchasing) power of this money inflow into the indefinite future. This time-machine function is known as *liquidity*. The possession of liquidity means that the person has sufficient money or other liquid assets that can be readily resold for money in an orderly, organized market to meet all his/her contractual obligations as they come due. In a world of uncertainty, a decision maker cannot know what contracts either already entered into, or will be entered into in the future, will be defaulted by the payer when the decision maker is the pay recipient. The decision maker also does not know if there will be a need for more money for him/her to discharge all future contractual obligations including some unexpected future contractual obligations as they come due.

Money is the liquid asset *par excellence*, for it can always settle any legal contractual obligation as long as the residents of the economy are law abiding and recognize the civil law of contracts. The more uncertain the decision maker feels about future economic events, the more money (or liquidity) he/she will desire to hold to meet possible unforeseen money contract contingencies. This characteristic of liquidity can be possessed in various degrees by some, but not all possible durables. Since any durable besides money can*not* (by definition) settle a contract, then for durables other than money to be a liquidity time machine they must have (1) low carrying costs and (2) low sales transaction costs by being easily salable in well-organized, orderly markets for money.[6]

The market for liquid financial assets must be well organized so as to have low transactions costs in bringing buyers and sellers together>. The market also must be orderly, i.e., any change in the market price from minute to minute must move in an orderly manner so that the next transaction price is not very different from the previous transaction price. As long as the market is orderly, the holder of liquid marketable securities believes he/she can make a fast exit by selling his/her holdings of the financial asset for money at a price not much different than the previously publically announced price.

The necessary condition for any market to be orderly is that there must be a market maker i.e., an institution possessing sufficient resources that it can and will make the market when there is a sudden absence of sufficient buyers (bulls) or sellers (bears). The market maker does not necessarily guarantee that the market price will never change over time. The market maker need only assure market participants that if the market price changes, it will change in an orderly manner, given the explicit, known rules under which the market maker operates.

For any liquid security asset the next moment's market price is never known with absolute certainty. What is known is that the price will not move in a disorderly manner from the last price because the market maker has sufficient liquidity to back up his/her assurance of an orderly market. For example, if suddenly many private sector holders of a specific financial asset suddenly turn bearish and try to make a fast exit from the market by selling their portfolio holdings, and, there are not enough buyers (bulls) to allow the bears to make an orderly exit from the financial market, then the market maker steps in and buys to maintain price movement orderliness in the market. If this private sector market maker's own resources are insufficient to maintain orderliness when there is a "herd behavior" rush to the exit, then trading is usually suspended via circuit breaker rules until the market maker can obtain sufficient resources to maintain orderliness and/or the selling panic subsides. If the private sector market maker cannot restore order in an important financial market, then it is the central banker who may have to become the *market maker of last resort* to either directly, or through providing resources to the market maker, restore orderliness.

A *fully liquid asset* is defined as any financial asset traded in a market where the private sector participants in the market 'know' that the market price in terms of monetary units will not change for the foreseeable future. To be a fully liquid asset, there must be a market maker who can guarantee that the money price of the asset will not change over time even if circumstances change. An example of a fully liquid asset is a foreign currency whose value in terms of domestic currency is fixed by the central bank of the nation. (As long as the central bank has sufficient foreign reserves, it can, if it wishes, guarantee a fixed exchange rate.)

A *liquid asset* is a durable asset with low carrying costs that is readily resalable in a well-organized, orderly market, but the market maker does not guarantee an unchanging market price. The market maker only assures market prices will change in an orderly manner.

An *illiquid asset* is an asset that cannot be readily resalable at any price in the market. Illiquid assets do not have orderly, organized resale markets. There is no market maker who is willing to organize an orderly market for the illiquid asset.

Two Essential Properties of Liquid Assets

As we have already suggested when decision makers save in the form of purchasing liquid assets that savings *per* se will not generate the market demand necessary to induce managers to hire workers to produce more goods and services. If this is correct then there are certain essential properties that liquid assets must possess if aggregate savings desired by the population in an economy is to have an effect on the level of employment and output in the economy. These essential properties that Keynes claimed are characteristic of all liquid assets and are the basis for differentiating Keynes's explanation of unemployment from the classical theory's explanation of unemployment that blames rigidities in market prices and/or money wages as the cause of unemployment. Keynes wrote "the Classical Theory has been accustomed to rest the supposedly self-adjusting character of the economic system on an assumed fluidity of money-wages, and where there is a rigidity, to lay on this rigidity the blame for maladjustment... My difference from this theory is primarily a difference of analysis."[7]

To explain unemployment due to a lack of sufficient market demand, Keynes identified two essential properties of money and all other liquid assets. Keynes stated: "The attribute of 'liquidity' is by no means independent of the presence of these two characteristics."[8] These two essential properties are:

1. all liquid assets are nonproducibles in the sense that even if the market demand for such assets increases, private sector business firms will not hire more workers to produce a greater supply of money or other liquid assets, and
2. there is no substitutability between liquid assets (including money) and reproducible goods to be used for storing savings for the purpose of providing liquidity necessary to purchase things at some future date.

Since money is the most liquid of all assets, essential property (1) means something that even pre-school children have to learn—namely that money does not grow on trees. Consequently, parents cannot just harvest a money tree to obtain more money when the child cries for purchasing an expensive toy in a store. Or as Keynes wrote: "money... cannot be readily reproduced;-labour cannot be turned on at will by entrepreneurs to produce money in increasing quantities as its price rises."[9] In other words, when the demand for money (liquidity) increases, private sector entrepreneurs cannot hire labor to produce more money (or any other liquid assets) to meet this increase in demand for these nonreproducible (by workers in the private sector) liquid assets.

Keynes's theory, defining savings as any portion of currently earned income that is not spent on produced goods and services. Accordingly the two essential properties Keynes identifies with money and all other liquid assets imply that as long as savers do not spend their accumulated savings on producibles, then these "resting" savings are denying other persons the ability to earn income by selling a producible to the saver for his/her savings.

Keynes demonstrated that the economy can find itself with significant levels of unemployment even in a competitive system with flexible wages and prices of producible goods and services whenever there are resting places for savings in nonproducibles. In other words, the belief that if market money wages were perfectly flexible rather than being rigid or even sticky there would be no unemployment is not true as long as liquidity is important factor in making market decisions and liquid assets have the aforementioned two essential properties that produce resting places for savings. The existence of such liquid assets which savers desire to use to store their savings indicates that any such nonreproducible asset allows income earners a choice between spending on employment inducing producible goods and services or spending one savings on liquid assets that and non-employment inducing demand.[10]

If a portion of income earned in producing goods and services is saved to be used to demand non-producible liquid assets, then unless others dissave, i.e., others spend on producibles sufficiently more than their income to offset the positive savings of today's savers, full employment cannot be achieved no matter how flexible are wages and prices of producibles.

In sum, if income earning savers store their savings in money and other liquid nonreproducible assets (that are *not* gross substitutes for the products of the capital goods producing industries), then all income earned by households engaging in the production of goods in any period is not, in the short or long run, necessarily spent on the products of industry. Households who want to store that portion of their income that they do not consume (i.e., that they do not spend on the products of industry) in liquid assets are choosing, a non-employment inducing demand for their savings. So it is the choice by savers of what to use to provide a resting place for their savings and not the rigidity or stickiness of wages and prices that can cause persistent levels of unemployment.

Apparently, Milton Friedman recognized this conceptualization of savings stored in the form of non-producibles as a problem for classical theory and the monetary economic analysis that he championed.

4 Unemployment: Why Can't People Who Want to Work Find Jobs?   51

Accordingly, Friedman implicitly resurrected the idea the free markets will insure full employment when he redefined the facts of what is consumption and especially what is "savings" in terms that should seem strange to most people.

Friedman does this by redefining consumption as "the value of services consumed" [utility] defines consumption as the complete using up of a purchased good. So, for example, if I purchase an ice cream pop from a seller on the street and then eat the pop, I have consumed the ice cream. Savings out of current income is then defined by Friedman as the portion of current income that is spent today to purchase producible durable goods. Since these goods are durables, they will not be completely used up immediately (consumed). Since, by definition a durable good will last for more than one day or one accounting period, then the total [utility] services derived from any durable purchased today cannot be, in Friedman's definition, completely consumed all in the one accounting day of purchase.

Consumption, in Friedman/s definition, involves the purchase of all nondurables during the accounting period (which, by definition of nondurable, means used up in the accounting period) plus the depreciation or utility used up, during the accounting period, of produced durables. Thus, in Friedman's theory of a monetary economy, today's purchase of long-lived producible durables such as cars, appliances, a diamond ring, a yacht, private airplane etc. in the current period are defined as savings out of current income (except for the slight depreciation of such a durable good during the current period).

Friedman claims his taxonomy is superior to others because "much that one classifies as consumption is reclassified as savings."[11] Accordingly Friedman can still maintain the assumptions of the known future and neutrality of money by redefining what people call savings. This new Friedman taxonomy suggests that the "facts" regarding what most people think as savings in the form of liquid assets that might support the Keynes analysis are wrong. When these "facts" about savings are redefined by Friedman, then the savings by households in terms of buying a newly produced durable out of current income create jobs just as much as household spending on nondurable consumption goods like food does in Friedman's model. Friedman's taxonomy presumes all income whether it is what he defines as savings or spent on consumption will be spent on the purchase of newly produced goods and services. Thus, savings creates jobs just as consumption spending does under the Friedman taxonomy!

Which concept of savings does the reader believe is more realistic? Is it Friedman's where a purchase of a new yacht is still defined as savings or Keynes's where the purchase of a yacht for pleasure boating is called consumption (or even conspicuous consumption by some)?

According to Keynes as long as savers rest their savings in nonproducibles assets and never use producible items as their place to store savings, then unemployment can occur even in the long run in an economic system with flexible wages and prices. Consequently, classical theory is never applicable to economy where money, money contracts, and liquidity are important determinants of people's actions in the marketplace of a money using system. Keynes's serious monetary and liquidity theory explains unemployment as the result of savings finding resting places in non-producible liquid assets where the desired level of aggregate savings by the population is not offset by equal dissavings (spending) of others in excess of their income in the same accounting period. Accordingly, whenever there is a significant strong aggregate propensity to save by savers in the form of liquid assets in the macroeconomy, there must be other decision makers willing to spend enough to dissave (go into debt?) if the economy is not to fall into recession.

Who are these dissavers likely to be? Keynes identified two basic important classes of dissavers—enterprises who finance their purchase of newly produced capital goods and inventories typically by borrowing from banks or by the issuing bonds and/or equities on the financial market, and governments who finance the buying costs of producible goods (infrastructure) and services in excess of tax revenues by borrowing, i.e., deficit spending.

Clearly the differing definition of savings and the lack of any concept of liquidity in Friedman's classical model of our economic system implies no need for the government deficit spending to ensure full employment since, under Friedman's redefinition of the facts household savings can only be via the purchase of producibles and therefore creates just as much demand for products produced by labor as consumption spending. Accordingly, as long as people spend all their income in each period on producibles there is no reason why the economy could not provide full employment as long as the government does not intervene in the market.

The Keynes analysis provides a differing rationale for the role of government policies that should be aimed at encouraging dissavings in the system to offset aggregate savings in order to end recessionary pressures in a modern economy.

Finally it is sometimes argued that unemployment occurs because the unemployed workers do not have the necessary skills need to fill a position offered by private sector employers. In this case, the unemployed workers are again blamed for their not being hired. If only the unemployed had pursued enough education they would have obtained sufficient skills to become employed.

But even that explanation is not sufficient. If market demand is sufficient, employers would provide on the job training for the unemployed to develop the skills necessary to produce profitable products for the enterprise. For example, during the Second World War, with many young men conscripted into the military, there were not enough men in the civilian population to fill all the "men's" jobs that the federal government's purchases of military equipment required. One of these men's jobs was that of riveters necessary to build ships for the Navy. Until then riveting was consider a job requiring physical strength only a man could do. With the shortage of available men to do this physical work, firms wanting to obtain lucrative government contracts successfully hired, and trained women to be riveters. These women were known as Rosie the Riveter. This example indicates that given sufficient market demand business firms can provide on the job training for those unemployed who presently apparently do not have enough skills for jobs required to meet market demands.

Notes

1. G. E. Moore, *Principia Ethica*, (Cambridge University Press, Cambridge, 1903).
2. R. F. Harrod, *The Life of John Maynard Keynes* (london, Macmillan, 1951) pp. 463–464.
3. J. M. Keynes, *The General Theory of Employment, Interest and Money*, (London, Macmillan, 1936) p. 210.
4. J. M. Keynes, *A Treatise on Money*, vol. 1, (Macmillan, London, 1930) pp. 3–4.
5. And even George Soros, "Letter to the Editor", *The Economist*, March 15–21, 1997 issue.
6. Even if an organized resale market exists for producible durable goods, these durable producibles typically have high carrying costs and high resale costs compared to money and other liquid financial assets. Accordingly producible durable goods are not the things in which people tend to store their savings. For example despite a market for second hand automobiles, savers do not store their savings out of current income via the purchase of an automobile.
7. *Op cit*, p. 257.
8. *Op cit*. p. 241 n.1.
9. *Op cit*. pp. 230.
10. *Op cit.*, p. 39.
11. *Op. Cit*, p. 28.

5

Creating a Prosperous Full Employment Economy

The fundamental cause of persistent unemployment in our market oriented economy is a shortage of market demand for all the goods and services our domestic industries can produce with a fully employed labor force. To avoid a state of persistent unemployment the government must develop policies that creates sufficient profitable market demand to encourage managers of domestic firms to hire all the unemployed workers who are looking for jobs.

To create the necessary market demand requires government policies that [1] encourages private sector households to spend more either by reducing their level of savings out of current total income and/or encourage business decision makers to borrow from banks to spend additional sums on investment in plant and equipment thereby encourage dissavings and/or [2] create more market demand spending by government deficit spending on producible projects that provide useful services for the population.

Monetary policy that reduces the interest rate on borrowing funds from the banking system may induce additional private sector borrowing by enterprises to purchase capital goods or even stock up on additional inventory in the belief that there will be additional spending in the near future by their customers. Unfortunately encouraging some forms of borrowing to induce additional private sector spending may not always encourage permanent good results. For example encouraging consumers in households where the breadwinner is already employed to spend more by increasing their credit card debt can create severe repayment problems for credit card holders. With the financial crisis many households lost jobs and incomes and thus faced increasing difficulties to meet their credit card payment obligations. The result can be an increase in credit card defaults and reduced total consumer spending.

Furthermore, after the financial crisis of 2007–2008, central banks such as the Federal Reserve reduced the basic interest on borrowing funds to practically a zero interest rate. The evidence indicates even at such a low interest rate, there was not enough additional borrowing by enterprises for investment purposes to generate a full employment economy. Monetary policy stimulus can be successful only if enough entrepreneurs have what Keynes called "animal spirits", i.e., optimistic expectations that market demand will occur in the near future at a sufficient rate to induce expectations that borrowing for additional investment spending currently will yield sufficient profits to service the resulting debt obligation.

Despite interest rates set by the Federal Reserve at near zero percent, for more than eight years after the global financial crisis, borrowing for investment spending by business has not been very large and the United States has been suffering through a "Great Recession". The lesson to be learned from this history is that monetary policy by itself may not be sufficient to rapidly revive our economy out of a significant recession. Enough deficit spending fiscal policy, however can always do the job.

Can a cut in personal income tax encourage additional spending by households? Obviously a reduction in the personal income tax rate will increase the after tax income of households that are still employed. The question is will an increase in after tax income encourage households to spend additional sums on the products of domestic industries. The immediate response would be that if household income after taxes increase they should be willing and even eager to spend some portion of this increase on goods and services.

Some classical economists, however, have argued that the cut in the tax rate will not encourage additional household spending. The immediate effect of the tax cut without any reduction in government spending will be to increase the government deficit and hence increase the outstanding government debt. Since, in classical theory, rational households have correct expectations about the future, some classical theorists have assumed that households will "know" this government debt must ultimately be paid off some time in the future. Consequently, these "rational" households will expect the government to raise taxes in the future to pay off its debt. Accordingly, this classical view argues that rational households will save their increases in after tax income in order to have sufficient funds to pay the higher future tax rates they expect the government to install to pay off the current deficit. Accordingly classical theory suggests that reducing income taxes may not stimulate additional household spending.

Keynes and Post Keynesian argue that given a tax reduction, some fraction of the increase in after tax income received by households will be spent on producible goods, while the remaining fraction of the increase in their after-tax income received will go to increase normal household savings for the unknown future. Accordingly, if instead cutting taxes to reduce total tax revenue by $X, the government adopts a policy to increase deficit spending on producible goods by the same $X as it would have returned to households as a tax cut, then the effect on the government deficit will be the same. But government direct spending will create more market demand for domestic production of goods and services than the stimulus of more market demand created by the reduction in personal income taxes since some portion of the additional after-tax income will be saved.

Moreover, in an economy open to imports, the question becomes will the spending by households out of their additional after tax income increase be entirely spent on domestically produced goods or will some of the increase in consumer spending be on imports that stimulate production and employment in foreign nations and therefore involve a smaller stimulus on domestic production.

In sum the Keynes analysis argues that a full employment economy in a market oriented system requires domestic business firms to recognize that they can expect enough market demand to profitably sell all they can produce with the capital and labor resources available in the economy. If private sector decision makers decide to save more (spend less) than they did in the previous period then enterprise will experience a decline in market demand and fewer workers will be employed.

To avoid this increase in unemployment, there must be other buyers of domestic production who decide to spend enough more to offset this hypothesized decline in market demand. It is unlikely that enterprises will borrow and spend more on new capital equipment when market demand is declining. Consequently to avoid this increase in unemployment it will be desirable for the federal government to spend more even though government must borrow and increase its outstanding debt to assure a more prosperous economy. After all a basic responsibility of government is to do whatever is possible to assure that the citizens of the nation are enjoying the most prosperous life possible with all who want to work to earn income can find employment.

Unfortunately some politicians think that the government faces the same budgetary constraints as does any individual household. These politicians declare that a rising public debt will ultimately bankrupt the nation. No economic topic has encouraged more political demagoguery than the claim that when a nation deficit spends, the effect is to result in an "unsustainable" growth in the total federal government's national debt that will ultimately lead to bankrupting the federal government. Those who proclaim this far of growing national debt are often labeled "deficit hawks".

These deficit hawks do not recognize that what is true for a household is not necessarily true for the nation. The economist John Kenneth Galbraith suggested the following advice to President Kennedy regarding responding to deficit hawks. Galbraith noted "One will always encounter the argument that the Federal Government should conduct its affairs like the average family and balance income and outgo.... the most useful answer to this is that the Federal Government, by unbalancing its budget, can help the man who needs a job to balance his budget".

A sage once said "Those who do not remember the past are doomed to repeat its errors". Deficit hawks clearly ignore the history of the United States national debt over the centuries.

As early as 1790, the newly founded United State government assumed the debts incurred by Congress during the Revolutionary

War. Thus from its very start the United States government accepted a national debt obligation that was a very large sum [$75 million] in those days.

In 1835, Andrew Jackson, the 7th president of the United States, submitted a budget that reduced government spending and was designed to pay off the national debt. Upon enactment of this Jackson debt payoff budget which significantly lowered government spending, the economy fell into a steep recession that last six years—and the national debt actually increased as tax revenues decreased more rapidly than government spending.

Since then the federal government had always had a significant outstanding dollar debt. During the First World War the national debt increased from approximately $4 billion in 1916 to $27 billion by 1919. The post-war prosperous 1920s saw a tremendous increase in private sector spending on producibles. The result was a full employment economy which generate significant large personal incomes. Annual tax receipts exceeded government spending and the total government debt was reduced 37% to $16.9 billion by 1929. During this often called "roaring twenties" era private sector spending increased sufficiently so there was no need for government to deficit spend to assure full employment. Consequently, the government actually ran a budget surplus and started to pay down the debt.

Private sector spending in the 1920s also was partly stimulated by the stock market bubble which increased the asset side of the balance sheet of most stock holders who as a result of the stock market rise, felt wealthier and therefore felt free to spend more out of current income. (The "irrational exuberance" of the dot.com bubble on the stock market of the 1990s had a similar effect in permitting government to run a budget surplus and reduce the national debt.)

When in 1929 private sector spending suddenly slowed and thereby reduced total market demand for the products of domestic industries, there was a drastic drop in business profits The United States entered the "Great Depression" and unemployment rose rapidly from 4.2% in 1928 to 23.8% in 1932. Tax revenues fell from $4 billion in 1930 to less than $2 billion in 1932. When President Roosevelt took office in 1933, the national debt had increased almost $20 billion, a sum equal to 33% of the nation's Gross Domestic Product and the unemployment rate was 25%.

During his first term in office, Roosevelt launched the "New Deal" that resulted in deficit spent large sums to build roads, schools, and other infrastructure projects. By 1936, the national debt had increased by 65% to $33 billion. This large increase in the national debt, however, was equal to only 40% of the Gross Domestic Product that had grown significantly from the depth of the Depression. Moreover, as a result of the New Deal's deficit spending the unemployment rate had declined from 25% in 1933 to 16.9% in 1936.

The Roosevelt Administration continued it deficit spending stimulus during the 1936 Presidential election year and unemployment continued to decline to a 14.3% by 1937. Nevertheless, many politicians and economic "experts" declared that the growth in the national debt was unsustainable. These people declared that disaster and possible bankruptcy awaited the nation if the government continued to deficit spend.

Accordingly, as part of his re-election campaign in 1936 Roosevelt promised to cut deficit spending. In 1937 Roosevelt delivered on his campaign pledge by submitting a budget to Congress that dramatically cut government spending. The result was the economy took a sharp downturn lasting through most of 1938. Unemployment jumped to 19% in 1938 as the economy fell into a steep recession with manufacturing output falling 37%. Tax revenue declined and the national debt increased to $37 billion. Before 1938 ended the Roosevelt Administration resumed significant deficit spending and the economy began to recover. By 1940 the economy had grown substantially while the national debt rose 16% to $43 billion (44% of the GDP) and the unemployment rate fell to 14.6%.

When the United States entered the Second World War at the end of 1941, the fear of deficits and national debt were forgotten. The important thing was to defeat the enemy by government purchasing as much military equipment as the armed services needed. By 1942 the unemployment rate fell to 4.7% as many young men were conscripted into the armed services and deficit spending for military equipment to fight the war increased dramatically. Between 1941 and the end of the war in 1945, GDP doubled while the national debt increased by more than

500% to $258 Billion. Most of the war spending was financed by government deficit borrowing rather than increasing taxes sufficiently to pay for the war. By 1945 the national debt was approximately 116% of the GDP.

Rather than bankrupting the nation, the large growth in the national debt promoted a prosperous economy. By 1946 the average American household was living much better economically than it had during the pre-war days. Moreover the children of the Depression and Second World War days were never burdened by having to pay off what was considered a huge national debt. In the 1950s, even the conservative Eisenhower Administration, launched the biggest peacetime public works project—the interstate highway system—rather than try to pay down the federal debt

The Kennedy and Johnson Administrations continued to spend large sums on sending a man to the moon and also on the escalating Vietnam war. As a result for more than two decades after World War 2, the United States experienced a golden age of economic growth and prosperity. The rich got richer while many of the poor experienced an even more a rapidly rising level of income that created a large American middle class.

The distribution of income became significantly less unequal. Large government deficit spending from the 1930s through the 1960s did not bring about an economic disaster. Instead it produced a continuous prospering market economy with a more equitable distribution of income and wealth. The history of the national debt and the economy from the Great Depression till the end of the 1960s was that the American economy had nothing to fear from running large government expenditure deficits. The federal government is the only buyer of producibles that can undertake the responsibility to dissave (deficit spend) to sufficiently increase the market demand for the products of domestic industries and therefore maintain a profitable entrepreneurial system which will give the opportunity for all who want to work to earn a living wage.

If the private sector will not spend enough to create sufficient market demand to permit all who want to work to gain a job, and if the fear of a large national debt keeps the federal government from deficit spending to create sufficient market demand, then the result will be impoverishing both domestic enterprises and workers. The basic Keynes message is our capitalist market system works best when spending causes a healthy growth in market demand and thereby generates profits and jobs and income for all the members of the community.

When the public and politicians recognize that a primary function of government fiscal policy is to act as a balancing wheel to assure that total market demand will be sufficient to encourage domestic entrepreneurs to create jobs for all the domestic workers, then we will have developed the political will to create a perpetual prosperous civilized economy. The next step will involve developing an international financial and payments system that will provide enough market demand to create a globally prosperous economy with full employment in every nation.

6

Can We Prevent Inflation and Still Achieve Full Employment?

Keynes's general theory analysis was developed in the 1930s after Britain had suffered more than a decade of high unemployment and depression—and not inflation. It is not surprising therefore that Keynes devoted most of his theoretical analysis in his general theory to curing the unemployment problem and relegated his discussion of changes in the price level to a single chapter in his general theory book.

Inflation becomes a serious problem when it reflects rising prices in many of the producible goods and services households purchase. Since the prices of producible are related to the costs of production of these goods and services, Keynes associated inflation with factors that caused the money costs of production to increase. Often inflation tends to occur when enterprises are increasing production levels and the economy in general is expanding. Keynes identified two main causes of a rising price level for new goods and services coming off the production line.

These are:

1. "Diminishing returns" or "bottlenecks" in production cause increasing production costs as firms tried to increase production output.

Diminishing returns inflation occurs when there is a real cost of expanding output in the sense that any expansion requires more labor time to produce the next unit of output than the amount of labor time necessary to produce the previous unit of output. Diminishing returns inflation involves a real increase in costs since it implies more labor effort is needed to produce the next unit of output as production flows expand.
2. Increase in the money "wage unit". In this case, any increase in the money wage rate per unit of labor time employed that is not offset by an increase in labor productivity that produces more output units per unit of labor time. This wage increase in excess of any increase in labor productivity means that every unit of produced output will be associated with increased labor costs compared to the labor costs per unit produced before the money wage rate increased.

Since Keynes had explicitly rejected the classical neutral money axiom in 1933,[1] his theory of inflation cannot be the classical quantitative theory of money where price level changes are directly associated with changes in the quantity of money relative to the level of produced output. Inflation in this classical quantity theory is solely the result of "too much money chasing too few goods". Consequently this classical quantitative theory suggests that the only cure for inflation is for the nation's central bank to limit the rate of growth of the supply of money to equal the rate of growth of produced output so that there is no change in the dollars available to chase the available goods. If central bankers believe in this quantitative theory of money and the price level, then to achieve if the central bank sets a target rate of inflation rate that the central bank believes desirable, say 2%, then monetary policy should increase the quantity of money 2% more rapidly than the rate of increase in the gross domestic product of the nation.

In Keynes's analysis money is never neutral in either the short-run or the long run. Consequently, Keynes's general theory suggests that when the economy is already at full employment the economy is producing the most goods and services it can. In Keynes's theory, only when the economy is already at full employment and domestic production of goods and services cannot be increased at all. If, at this point, an increase in the money supply that induces an increase spending on domestically produced goods and services occurs, then the result in inflation.

The Keynes–Post Keynesian theory suggests that whenever there is persistent unemployment in the system the proper target of central bank monetary policy is (1) to create and maintain sufficient liquidity in the system and (2) to encourage dissaving (borrowing) by private sector decision makers in the hopes they will spend the borrowed funds to purchase additional products from domestic industries. If this easy monetary policy does create an increased market demand, this will encourage enterprises to hire more workers.

To rely solely on the central bank to stop inflation from occurring will require the central bank to sufficiently constrain borrowing to buy products so that either (1) enterprise does not produce in the range of diminishing returns, or (2) market demand for production is held back so there is enough unemployment in the system to remove the bargaining power of workers to demand increases in money wages that exceed any increases in labor productivity in the industry.

As early as 1930, Keynes wrote that bank "credit is the pavement along which production travels, and the bankers if they knew their duty, would provide the transport facilities to just the extent that is required in order that the productive powers of the community can be employed at their full capacity".[2] As long as the economy is at less than full employment, the central bank pursue an "easy monetary policy" should be designed to encourage banks to make more loans available to borrowers, who will use these loans to purchase products such as new plant and equipment and, newly built, housing. This will increase employment until the economy, obtains and maintains full employment. In other words, the primary function of a central bank, as controller of the banking system, is to encourage bankers to make credit (liquidity) available as cheaply as possible to those who want to borrow to buy more goods and services in the marketplace and who have sufficient income and/or collateral to service the resulting debt obligations. As long as the economy has significant idle labor resources that could be gainfully employed, monetary policy should facilitate spending to encourage economic expansion and growth. If money is not neutral, then the central bank's function should not be to set a target for the observed rate of price level inflation before full employment is achieved.

If the economy is at less than full employment while inflation is occurring at a rate that the central bank believes is undesirable, then the only way the central bank can attempt to reduce this observed inflation rate is if it increases interest rates and restricts bank credit availability to private sector borrowers. This anti-inflation monetary policy can work if it reduces aggregate market demand sufficiently if encourages entrepreneurs to reduce production that either (1) depresses production below the area where diminishing returns occurs, or (2) if the lower market demand induces employers to reduce the number of workers they hire. This reduction in demand for labor then may reduce the power of labor to demand higher wages and therefore reduce the pressure of rising labor production costs to increase the level of prices.

Since production of output takes time, if market demand is increasing bottlenecks can occur that prevents a rapid increase in production reaching the market for some period of time. Thus if there is a sudden increase in the market demand for products for immediate delivery, this spot market demand can only be met by sales out of existing inventory and the size of available inventory can become a bottleneck that prevents delivery to all buyers who want immediate access to the product. There is nothing the central bank can do to stop this type of lack of sufficient inventory to meet immediate spot price inflation.

Contracts, Prices and Inflation

Our earlier discussion of the importance of money and the use of spot and forward contracts provides us with the platform for explaining the cause(s) of inflation in the real world and the policies possible to constrain inflationary tendencies. In all modern money-using economies, all market production and exchange transactions are organized via money contracts in either a spot market or a forward market. Accordingly, at any point of calendar time, there may exist simultaneously two prices for ant producible good. These two prices are (1) the spot price for immediate delivery and (2) the forward price that is today's contractual agreed on price to pay at a specific future date (or dates) when product delivery and payment are contractually agreed upon. Since production takes some period of calendar time before the final goods can appear in the market, the spot price for a product will deal with commodities already produced and are currently being held in inventory for immediate sale on the market. Forward prices will be associated with goods whose production will begin if the buyer is willing to enter a contractual order to receive delivery when the product is finished and comes off the end of the production line.

Alfred Marshall, the teacher of Keynes and a famous economist in his own right, noted that spot market prices could be at any level that cleared the market for instant delivery. The spot price is a price where every unit of existing output is willingly held by some person or business firm either to use the product immediately or to hold in inventory for sale in the future—even if the spot price does not cover the costs of production incurred in producing this inventory. On the other hand, the forward or short-run price is the offer price of sellers that buyers must be willing to accept in order to place a forward contractual order. With that forward contractual order in hand, the seller will undertake the necessary productive activity to assure the product will be available for delivery at the specific forward contractual future date. In other words, all forward prices are associated with the necessary money costs of production (including profits) that are required to be paid to the business firm to encourage entrepreneurs to hire enough productive inputs to achieve a specific production output target at a specific point of time. It should be noted that in our world of experience, it is a stylized fact that except at the retail level, almost all production is related to forward contractual orders received by the producer-seller.

In his earlier *Treatise on Money*,[3] Keynes had identified two types of inflation (and deflation): *Commodity Inflation (or Deflation)* and *Incomes Inflation (or Deflation)*. Commodity inflation was identified with rising spot market prices over time where at any immediate point of time only pre-existing stocks of goods in inventory can be sold on the market. Since production takes some duration of calendar time to occur, if there is a sudden increase in spot market demand for products, there can be no available augmentation of existing stocks for immediate delivery to constrain this spot market inflation. The immediate result is a commodity spot price inflation. (If commodity inflation has occurred, then holders of the pre-existing durable producibles can sell their inventory at a higher spot price than previously and thereby obtain a capital gain on their holdings.)

The second form of inflation, *Incomes Inflation*, is associated with rising prices that are associated with increases in the money costs of production and/or profit margin associated with each unit of goods produced. These money costs of production represent the income payments to wage and salary earners, material suppliers, lenders, and profit recipients. In other words, if the money costs per unit of production increase and are being paid, then owners of at least some of the inputs to the production process are receiving higher money incomes.

One of the most widely used forward contracts is the labor hiring contract where entrepreneurs agree to pay workers a specified money wage per hour, or per week or even per annum for the duration of the labor contract.

This incomes inflation taxonomy highlights the obvious but oft neglected fact that, given productivity relations, inflationary increases in the prices of domestic producible goods are always associated with (and the result of) an increase in some domestic resident's money income earned in the production process. Often this incomes inflation is associated with increases in the money wages paid workers via a forward labor hiring contract. If this wage increase is greater than any productivity increase per worker then the costs of production must have risen. Accordingly if the nation is to adopt a policy of achieving a constraint on the rate of incomes inflation of domestically producible goods, one must somehow have a policy—an incomes policy—which constrains the rise in the money income of owners of inputs, often typically wage rates since labor costs are usually a major cost of production.

The Inflation Process in a Keynes World

Spot prices, by definition, move in step with immediate changes in the market demand for immediate delivery of existing products. Thus, at any moment in calendar time every unexpected sudden increase in demand for products and/or services for immediate delivery can produce an increase in spot prices. While a fall in market demand for immediate delivery will result in a commodity price deflation.

It is, however, the effect on forward—not spot—prices that is most important for explaining a continuing (over calendar time) inflation problem with the prices of goods and services that most households buy. No matter how high spot prices go at any point of calendar time, if forward prices (and therefore costs of production) remain stable, then if buyers are willing to wait the gestation period for the production of additional output, buyers can always order today newly produced goods and services for delivery at a future date at today's forward (supply) price offering by enterprises. If, despite any hypothetical increase in spot demand, the costs of production and therefore the forward prices remain stable over time, then the spot price inflation can only be a temporary (market period) phenomena that will be diminished when additional finished product is available for sale in the spot market place. Moreover to the extent that the spot price of commodities with long gestation periods are the inflation problem, and there is no spill-over causing a rise in the money costs of new production, then the policy solution for this spot price inflation is the holding by the government of buffer stocks.

Buffer stocks since a spot or commodity price inflation occurs whenever there is a sudden and unforeseen change in demand or available supply *for immediate delivery*, this type of inflation can easily be avoided if there is some institution that is not motivated by self-interest but instead maintains a "buffer stock" to prevent unforeseen changes in spot demand and supply from inducing significant spot price movements. A buffer stock is nothing more than some commodity shelf-inventory that can be moved into and out of the spot market to buffer the market from disorderly price disruptions by offsetting the unforeseen changes in spot demand or supply.

For example, since the oil price shocks of the 1970s, the United States government has developed a "strategic petroleum reserve". The government bought crude oil in the market and stored these crude oil inventories in underground salt domes on the coast of the Gulf of Mexico. These strategic petroleum reserves were designed to be held in inventories to provide emergency market oil supplies to buffer the domestic oil spot market if there is a sudden decrease in oil supplies from the politically unstable Middle East that threatens to encourages additional speculative demand for oil on the spot oil commodity market. The strategic use of such a petroleum reserve means that the spot price of oil will not increase as much as it otherwise would if, for example, a political crisis broke out in the Middle East. Spot oil price inflation could be avoided as long as the buffer stock exists to offset any potential threatening immediately available commodity shortage. For example, during the short Desert Storm war against Iraq in 1991, US government officials made strategic petroleum reserves available to the commodity oil market to offset the possibility of disruptions (actual or expected) from affecting the spot price of crude oil. The Department of Energy estimated that this 1991 use of the strategic petroleum reserve as a buffer stock during the brief Desert Storm period prevented the price of gasoline at the pump from rising about 30 cents per gallon.

Use of buffer stocks as a public policy solution to spot price inflation or deflation is as old as the biblical story of Joseph and the Pharaoh's dream of seven fat cows followed by seven lean cows. Joseph—the economic forecaster of his day—interpreted the Pharaoh's dream as portending seven good harvests where production would be much above normal and market prices (and therefore farmers' incomes) will be below normal; followed by seven lean harvests where production would not provide enough food to go around while prices farmers received would be exorbitantly high. Joseph's civilized policy proposal for avoiding inflation and deflation in food prices was for the government to build up and store a *buffer stock* of grain during the good years and release the grain to market to be sold without government profit, during the bad years. This would maintain a stable price over the fourteen harvests and avoiding inflation in the bad years while protecting farmer's incomes in the good harvest years. The Bible records that this civilized buffer stock policy to stabilize commodity prices and farmers' income over a period of fourteen harvests was a resounding economic success.

Incomes Inflation

Increases in money wages, salaries and other material costs in production contracts always imply the increase in someone's money income. The costs of production of a firm are the other side of the coin of the income of people who provide labor or other resources for use by the firm in the production process. A cost of production always represents someone's income!

With slavery illegal in civilized societies, the money-wage contract for hiring labor is the most universal of all production costs. Labor cost accounts for the vast majority of production contract costs in the economy, even for such high-technology products as NASA spacecraft. That is why, especially during the first four decades after the Second World War, consumer price inflation was usually associated with money-wage increases.

Wage contracts specify a certain money-wage per unit of time over the duration of the contract. This labor cost plus a profit margin or mark-up to cover material costs, overheads, and profit on the investment become the basis for managerial decisions as to the prices they must receive on a forward sales contract to make the undertaking worthwhile in terms of covering costs and returning a profit. If money wages rise relative to the productivity of labor, then the labor costs of producing each unit of outputs increase. Consequently firms must raise their sales (forward) contract price if they are to maintain profitability and viability. When any production costs per unit of output are increasing, then forward contract prices for orders for produced goods and services are rising throughout the economy. The economy is suffering a forward contract or *incomes inflation*.

To prevent incomes inflation there must be some constraint on the rate of increase of money incomes relative to productivity. This requires some form of incomes policy.

Incomes Policy

For several decades after the Second World War money wage rates were increasing faster than labor productivity in most developed nations. This was a major factor in the Incomes Inflation these nations experienced. To understand why this was so prevalent at that time, we must recognize the change in the nature of the industrial society that came after the Second World War. As John Kenneth Galbraith noted; "The market with its maturing of industrial society and its associated political institutions…loses radically its authority as a regulatory force…[and] partly it is an expression of our democratic ethos."[4]

After the devastating loss of income experienced by most households during the Great Depression of the 1930s, the emerging ethos of the common man in democratic nations held that people should have more control of their economic destiny. The Great Depression had taught that individuals cannot have control of their economic lives if they leave the determination of their income completely to the tyranny of the free market. Consequently after World War II in societies with any democratic tendencies people not only demanded economic security from their economic system but they also demanded to play a controlling role in determining their economic life. This required power to control one's income. The result was an institutional power struggle for higher money incomes between unions, political coalitions, economic cartels and monopolistic industries. When these power struggles lead to demands for higher incomes at any level of production, the result is Incomes Inflation.

As long as the government guarantees that it will pursue a full employment policy, then each self-interested worker, union, and business entrepreneur has less to fear that their demand for higher prices and money income will result in a significant loss in sales resulting in earning less income and unemployment. As long as the government accepts the responsibility for creating sufficient aggregate effective demand to maintain the economy close to a full employment level of output, there may be no market incentive to stop this recurring struggle over the distribution of income when all available resources are being utilized.

Full employment policies assures that there would no longer exist what Marx called "the industrial reserve army" of the unemployed to constrain the demands of employed workers for higher wages. In a laissez-faire market environment, employers are free to choose to hire workers from the pool of unemployed to replace workers currently employed. In this free market system, a significantly large industrial reserve army of the unemployed can be a major force that constrains organized workers' demand for higher money wages. If the government assures a persistent full employment policy what is to constrain workers from persistently demanding higher money wages?

In an open economy where free trade exists and multinational enterprises make important decisions regarding where geographically production is to take place, foreign workers who earn wages significantly below that of domestic workers can act as the equivalent of a Marxian "industrial reserve army" to keep domestic money wages constrained and even many domestic workers unemployed. Since the 1990s, with a continuous push for globalized free trade, the almost unlimited supply of unskilled and semi-skilled workers in countries such as China and India willing to work at much lower wages than those that prevail in the West have acted similar to a Marxist "industrialized army of the unemployed" in limiting western workers ability to even maintain, on average, the existing money wage rate. (We will discuss possible policy solutions for this problem of outsourcing production to emerging economies with low paid workers in the following chapters.) Consequently, by the beginning of the twenty first century, the threat of runaway high rates of incomes inflation due to inflationary money wage increases have fallen off the radar screen of most OECD nations. In fact, price deflation has become a depressing factor in some western developed nations.

For those classical economists who believe in the beneficence of the "invisible hand" of free markets, there is only one way to combat any incomes inflation that may occur in our economy. In a free society where people are motivated solely by self-interest, workers and entrepreneurs are free to organize to demand a higher price for their services, even if such demands are inflationary. As the former Prime Minister of England, Mrs. Thatcher, was often quoted as warning "One of the rights of a free society is the right to price oneself out of the market".

In the decades immediately after the Second World War, to restrain inflationary wage demands often by unionized workers and entrepreneurs lacking significant competition in the market place, a policy where the nation's central bank constrained the banking system from providing all the working capital finance necessary to pay these inflationary income demand was thought to be the "only game in town: The resulting lack of sufficient effective market demand did sometimes create situations where those demanding higher money incomes were, as Mrs. Thatcher had stated, often priced out of the market.

If an independent central bank adamantly refuses to increase the money supply sufficiently to finance inflationary income demands of owners of domestic factors of production, then the resultant slack demand in the market place for domestic goods and services can discipline all workers and firms with the fear of loss of sales and income. The hope is that this fear will keep wage and price demand increases in check. To make this fear credible, central banks have adopted a policy of telling the public that they have a target of some inflation rate. If the observed inflation rate exceeds the central bank's target, then the central bank implies that it will institute a restrictive monetary policy sufficiently "tight" to reduce market demand so that domestic enterprises feel threatened with loss of profitable market conditions while workers feel threatened with unemployment Nothing closely approaching full employment prosperity can be tolerated as long as we rely on the central bank's free market incomes policy of threatening workers with unemployment and enterprise with falling profit levels. Thus those who advocate that central banks publically announce a low "inflation target" on which the monetary policy will depend are implicitly endorsing an incomes policy based on creating fear expectations of loss of jobs, sales revenues, and profits for enterprises that produce goods and services domestically. An incomes policy of FEAR, it is believed, will keep owners of the domestic factors of production in their place. The amount of slack demand necessary to enforce this *incomes policy of fear* will depend on what is some modern classical economists call the domestic *natural rate of unemployment*. This natural rate is defined as the necessary rate of unemployment which prevents workers to demand increases in money wages that exceed increases in labor productivity and therefore create wage-price inflation.

Accordingly, proponents of this inflation targeting incomes policy of fear are implicitly suggesting that the natural unemployment rate will be smaller if government "liberalizes" labor markets by reducing, if not completely eliminating long-term unemployment benefits or other money income supports including minimum wages, employer contributions to pension funds, employer provided health insurance for their employees, legislation protecting working conditions, etc. The belief is that workers will be less truculent and more willing to accept the existing wage structure when the government removes unemployment benefits and other support policies.

To those who advocate such an incomes policy of fear, a permanent large social safety net is seen as mollycoddling casualties in the war against inflation so that others may think there is little to fear if they join the ranks of the unemployed. A ubiquitous and overwhelming fear instilled in all members of society is a necessary condition for the barbarous inflation targeting program to work in a period of undesirably high rates of inflation. The result is inevitably that the civil society is the first casualty.

With the integration of populous nations such as China, India, etc into the global economy of the twenty first century, as we have already suggested, another "industrial reserve army" has been introduced into the economies of many OECD nations. Since the 1990s, with the almost unlimited supply of idle and unemployed workers (often including children) in these populous nations who are eager to accept jobs at wages much below those prevailing in the major OECD nations and the growing phenomena of outsourcing of manufacturing jobs and services incomes, the labor forces of major industrial nations have been significantly constrained in their wage income demands. As a result incomes inflation has been limited to those domestic service occupation and industries and manufacturing industries (e.g., national defense) where outsourcing is not a possible alternative and the unemployment rate in the industry is relatively low.

As cheap foreign workers have often replaced higher paid domestic labor in many production processes, enterprise profit margins have been increasing. The result has been significant increases in the profit share of income, often leading to large increases in the income of senior managers and owners of many business enterprises. The result has been a growing inequality of income between the unskilled, semi-skilled and even some skilled workers in Western Industrial nations and the domestic managers and owners of multinational corporations who can engage in outsourcing of their lower end jobs and demanding higher profit margins on the segment of their integrated chain that provide goods and services domestically.

What civilized anti-inflation incomes policy can one develop from Keynes's revolutionary analytic approach? In 1970, Sidney Weintraub, basing his analysis on Keynes's analytical framework[5] developed a "clever" anti-inflation policy which he called TIP or a tax-based incomes policy.[6] TIP required the use of the corporate income tax structure to penalize the largest domestic firms in the economy if they agreed to wage rate increases in excess of some national productivity improvement standard and/or if the firms raised prices to increase profit margins significantly. Thus the tax system would be used to penalize those firms that agreed to inflationary wage demands or profit mark ups. The hope of TIP was that if wage increases could be limited to overall productivity increases, then workers and owners of all other inputs to the domestic production process would willing accept non-inflationary monetary income increases. Increases in real incomes of the owners of the factors of production would then be associated with increases in productivity.

There were two conditions that Weintraub believed were necessary if TIP was to be an effective policy that did not rely on "fear" of loss of income to constrain Incomes Inflation. These conditions were:

a. TIP was to be a permanent policy institution, and
b. TIP must be a penalty system, not a reward (subsidy) tax system.

Once instituted, TIP could never be removed for otherwise it would become an impotent policy as it reached its termination date. Weintraub indicated that the magnitude of the tax penalties could be altered as conditions warranted, but there must always be the existence of a threat of penalties to insure compliance.

Secondly, a reward tip, i.e., one which reduced people's taxes if they adhered to the national wage standard would be administratively unworkable, as everyone would claim the reward and it would be up to the government to prove which claimants were not entitled to the reduction in taxes. Weintraub suggested that TIP was similar to the way government enforces speed limits on the nation's highways. If one exceeds the speed limit—which is always in place—one paid a speeding fine. Governments never paid good drivers for not exceeding the speed limit.

Unfortunately, the United States and many other nations have never seriously attempted to develop a permanent penalty-oriented TIP. Instead in the last decades of the twentieth century inflation was typically fought via the typical Monetarist "incomes policy of fear" i.e., restricting the growth of the money supply so as to create slack labor markets via recession. Those who raise their wages above productivity growth will then find themselves priced out of the marketplace.

The real cost of such a Monetarist incomes policy to many industrialized nations in the last decades of the twentieth century was significant. For countries such as Germany and France, double digit unemployment rates—previously unseen since the Great Depression—became the norm.

Only in recent decades has the problem of inflationary wage demand been almost eliminated by enterprises "outsourcing" jobs to production plants in foreign nations. This outsourcing by management forces the remaining employed domestic workers to accept stagnant wage rates while being sufficiently thankful that their jobs have not been outsourced.

Weintraub, the perpetual believer in the use of human intelligence rather than brute (market) forces to encourage socially compatible civilized behavior, believed that ultimately some form of civilized incomes constraint policy would be seen as a more humane policy to control inflation without the necessary depressing side effects of traditional Monetarist policy.

In the following chapters on International trade, a policy will be suggested that permits a developed nation's labor force to be protected from the "industrial reserve army" of the cheap foreign labor nations and thereby provide the hope for maintaining full employment of the domestic labor force. At that time when government introduce policies to protect domestic workers from the competition of this foreign industrial reserve army, the nation may simultaneously have to introduce a civilized incomes policy such as TIP to constrain inflationary income demands of domestic owners of the inputs into the domestic production processes as the threat of foreign cheap labor competition is reduced.

Words and concepts are important weapons in the fight against inflation. One of the most important functions of government in any anti-inflationary struggle is to educate the public of the major industrialized nations that the income distribution struggle is (in the aggregate) an uncivilized no-win game. Although there may be some relative winners for periods of time, the basic civil instincts of the nation's society will be the ultimate loser. In the absence of a sensible policy about the distribution of income nationally and internationally, the result is not a zero-sum game, but a real loss in total aggregate income nationally and internationally as governments compete via pursuing restrictive monetary and/or "austerity" fiscal policies to reduce outstanding debt obligations both domestically and, as we will discuss, international debts among nations.

Notes

1. J. M. Keynes, "A Monetary Theory of Production" (1933) reprinted in *The Collected Writings of John Maynard Keynes, 13*, edited by D. Moggridge, (London, Macmillan, 1973).
2. J. M. Keynes, *A Treatise on Money, vol. 2*, (Macmillan, London, (1930), p. 220.

3. J. M. Keynes, *A Treatise on Money*, vol. 1, (Macmillan, London, 1930) reprinted as *The Collected Writings of John Maynard Keynes*, vol. 5, edited by D. Moggridge (Macmillan, London, 1971) reprint, p. 140.
4. J. K. Galbraith, "On Post Keynesian Economics", *Journal of Post Keynesian Economics, 1*, pp. 8–9.
5. S. Weintraub, *An Approach to the Theory of Income Distribution*, (Chilton, Philadephia, 1958).
6. S. Weintraub, "An Incomes Policy to Stop Inflation" *Lloyds Bank Review*, 1971.

7

The Role of Financial Markets and Liquidity

The winter of 2007–2008 proved to be a winter of discontent in global financial markets. Initially the United States subprime mortgage problem created an insolvency problem for major underwriters. The exotic financial instruments that they created such as mortgage backed derivatives lost liquidity and market value. This problem proved contagious as it spilled over to other exotic financial markets such as the auction-rate securities markets[1] and the credit default swap markets.[2]

Alan Greenspan reflected the view of most well-known mainstream economists when, in his congressional testimony, he stated that he did not foresee the coming of the global financial crisis and could not explain why it occurred using well established mainstream economic theory including some Nobel Prize economic analysis. The facts were the United States subprime mortgage problem created an insolvency problem for major underwriters. The exotic financial instruments that these institutions created such as mortgage backed derivatives lost liquidity and market value. This problem proved contagious as it spilled over to other financial markets such as the auction-rate securities markets and the credit default swap markets.

The auction-rate markets, which had seen few failures in years, suddenly experienced over a thousand failures in the early months of 2008. What caused this contagion to spill over and what was the cause for this tremendous increase in market failures?

The answer is simple. Economists and market participants had forgotten Keynes's liquidity preference theory and had, instead swallowed hook, line, and sinker the belief that the classical efficient financial market theory is the useful model for understanding the operation of real world financial markets. This efficient market theory indicates that all one has to do is to bring informed buyers and sellers together in an unregulated, free financial market and the resulting financial market price will always adjust in an orderly manner to a price reflecting the known future value of the underlying assets. This known future was obtained by analyzing readily available existing information called market "fundamentals" such as price/earnings ratios, risks of defaults, etc. These fundamentals is information readily available to all via modern computer reporting of market trends and history of market behavior in the past.

Bringing the buyers and sellers of financial securities together, however, requires providing a place for a well-organized and orderly financial market where trading between buyers and sellers can readily take place. In the pre-computer age, financial markets required buyers and sellers to be represented by broker–dealers who would meet in a physical location (e.g., the stock exchange) to engage in trades. The dealers who were members of these financial asset market exchanges recognized that at any given moment of the trading day, there may be a problem of getting a sufficient number of bona fides buyers and sellers together to maintain an orderly market.

For the market to be well-organized it was necessary to adopt financial market rules that required all market participants to deal only with authorized broker–dealers that were permitted to execute trades in the specific market place. The broker–dealers acted as fiduciary agents for specific buyers or sellers to place orders with other members of the stock exchange, sometimes called "specialists". Each specialist kept the books on all buy and sell orders for a specific security at any price. If, for example, at any time during the trading day, the number of sellers heavily outweighed the number of buyers at the last trade price, then to provide an orderly market price change from the previous trade price, the specialist was expected to act as a "market maker" and buy on his/her own account to limit the decline in price to a small orderly change from the previous transaction price. If, on the other hand, the number of buy orders far exceeded the number of sell orders. Then the market maker would sell from his own portfolio in order to maintain an orderly increase in market price.

Orderliness is a necessary condition to convince holders of the market traded financial asset that they can readily sell (liquidate) for money their portfolio holdings of a specific security at a market price at, or near, the last transaction price. In other words, orderliness is necessary to maintain the belief in liquidity in these markets.

Modern financial efficient market theory suggests that these quaint institutional arrangements for market maker specialists are antiquated in this computer age. The computer can keep the book on buy and sell order, and, it is claimed, the computer can match buy and sell orders and therefore maintain orderliness. With the computer and the internet, there will be huge numbers of buyers and sellers meeting rapidly and efficiently in virtual space. Consequently there is no need for humans to act as specialist market makers to keep the books and to assure the public the market is orderly as well as well-organized.

Underlying this efficient market view of the role of financial markets is the presumption that the current and future value of traded financial assets is already predetermined by today's market "fundamentals" (at least in the long run[3]). Former US Treasury Secretary and Harvard Professor Lawrence Summers has written that financial markets are efficient in that their "ultimate social functions are spreading risks, guiding investment of scarce capital, and processing and dissemination the information possessed by diverse traders....*prices always reflect fundamental values* .... The logic of efficient markets is compelling"[4].

In the numerous financial markets that became disorderly and failed in the Winter of 2007–2008, the underlying financial instruments that were to provide the future cash flow for investors typically involved long term debt instruments such as mortgages, or long-term corporate or municipal bonds. A necessary condition for these markets to be efficient is that the probabilistic risk of the debtors to fail to meet all future cash flow contractual debt obligations can be "known" to all market participants with actuarial certainty. With this actuarial knowledge, it even can be profitable for insurance companies to sell credit default swaps insurance to holders of these financial debt instruments guaranteeing the holder would be reimbursed for remaining interest payments and principal repayment at maturity if a default did occur.

In the efficient market theory, any observed market price variation around the actuarial value (price) of the traded liquid security assets representing these debt instruments in the aforementioned markets is presumed to be statistical "white noise". Any statistician will tell you, if the size of the sample increases, then the variance (i.e., the quantitative measure of the white noise) decreases. Since computers can bring together many more buyers and sellers globally than the antiquated pre computer market arrangements, therefore, at any point of time the size of the sample of trading participants in the computer age will rise dramatically. If, therefore, you believe in the efficient market theory, then permitting computers to organize the market will decrease significantly the variance and therefore increase the probability of a more well organized and orderly market than existed in the pre-computer era.

Consequently, efficient market theory advocates such as Summers suggest that the spreading of probabilistic risks for holders of these assets is much more efficient while the cost of each transaction is diminished significantly as computers take over for human order keepers. Underlying the efficient market theory, however, is a fundamental presumption namely that the future is known and can be predicted on the basis of historical data. This presumes there exists an unchanging probability distribution governing past, present, and future events. Available information of market fundamentals are represented by historical data. Thus if the probability distribution which is presumed to govern the past, is also the same probability distribution that will govern the future, then historical data provide useful fundamental information regarding future earnings, payments, etc. If one accepts the classical assumption that the future is knowable and predictable then as Summers states "The logic of efficient market theory is compelling".

For believers in classical based efficient market theory, the presumption that, at any moment in time, there is a plethora of market participants buyers and sellers that can be collected by a computer assures that the assets being traded are very liquid. In a world of efficient financial markets, holders of market traded assets can readily liquidate their position at a price close to the previously announced market price whenever any holder wishes to reduce his/her position in that asset. If the efficient market theory is applicable to our world, then how can we explain that in 2007–2008 so many securitized financial markets failed in the sense that "investors are finding themselves locked into investments they can't cash out of"?[5]

Keynes's liquidity preference theory can provide the explanation. Keynes' liquidity theory presumes that the economic future is uncertain and not actuarially predictable. Consequently, efficient market theory is not applicable to real world financial markets. Keynes's analysis presumes that, in the real world of experience, the past activity of the macroeconomic and financial systems are not reliable guides to the probability of future outcomes.

If future outcomes cannot be reliably predicted on the basis of existing past and present data, then there is no actuarial basis for insurance companies to provide holders of financial assets protection against unfavorable outcomes. Accordingly, it should not be surprising that insurance companies such as AIG that wrote credit default swap insurance policies to protect asset holders against possible unfavorable outcomes found themselves experiencing billions of dollars more in losses than the insurance companies had previously estimated.[6] In financial markets, it is impossible to develop insurance premiums that will cover estimated insurance payouts in the future. Nor will there be available "fundamentals" data providing market participants with an actuarial correct outlook about the future value of these financial instruments.

In our uncertain economic world, the primary function of financial markets that trade in resalable securities is to provide a place to store savings that possess liquidity. The degree of liquidity of the assets traded in any organized market will be enhanced by the existence of a credible market maker. As previously stated, a market maker is someone who attempts to create public confidence in the belief that there will always be an orderly resale market. In other words, in a market where a market maker exists holders of the asset can be reasonable confident that they can always execute a fast exit strategy and liquidate their position in the asset at a market price that is very close to the last publically recorded price. In essence, the market maker suggests to holders that if buyers do not appear to purchase offered securities at an orderly decline in price, then the market maker will make his/her best efforts to maintain orderliness even if this requires the market maker to buy, for his/her own account, the securities offered for sale. If the market maker cannot support his/her assurance to maintain orderliness with sufficient cash when a cascade of sell orders come onto the market, then the market will fail, and the asset becomes virtually illiquid as trading will be suspended until the market maker can rally enough additional support for the buyers' side of the market to reinstate orderliness. This suspension of trading if temporary in a well organized market that is orderly is typically called a "circuit breaker".

In other words, for an orderly liquid resale market to exist, *there must be a creditable "market maker"* who assures the public that he/she will swim against any rip-tide of sell (or buy) orders. The market maker must therefore be very wealthy, or at least have access to significant quantities of cash if needed. Nevertheless, any private market maker could exhaust his/her cash reserve in fighting against a cascade of sell orders from holders. Liquidity can be guaranteed under the harshest of market conditions *only* if the market maker has easy direct or indirect access to the Central Bank to obtain all the funds necessary to maintain financial market orderliness. Only market makers having such preferred access to the Central Bank can be reasonably certain they *always* can obtain enough cash to stem any potential disastrous financial market collapse.

An interesting illustration of this market maker exercise occurred on the days following the terrorist attacks on the World Trade Center and the Pentagon on September 11, 2001. As the World Trade Center buildings collapsed there was a great fear that public confidence in New York financial markets and the United States government would also collapse. To maintain confidence in the U.S. government bond market, in the two days following the attack, the Federal Reserve pumped $45 billion into the banking system. Simultaneously, since the primary bond dealers in New York tend to "make" the U.S. government bond market, "to ease cash concerns among primary dealers in bonds—which include investment banks that aren't able to borrow money directly from the Fed—the Fed on Thursday [September 13, 2001] snapped up all the government securities offered by dealers, $70.2 billion worth. On the next day it poured even more into the system, buying a record $81.25 billion of government securities"[7]. In effect, these actions of the Federal Reserve removed securities from the general public by making the market and providing easily available liquidity to financial intermediaries. These intermediaries could then also make the market by exercising purchases of all government bonds offered by members of the general public who wanted to make a fast exit.

Furthermore, The *Wall Street Journal* reported that just before the New York Stock Exchange reopened on September 17 for the first time after the World Trade Center attack, investment banker Goldman Sachs, loaded with liquidity due to Fed activities, phoned the chief investment officer of a large mutual fund group to tell him that Goldman was willing to buy any stocks the mutual fund managers wanted to sell. The *Journal* noted that, at the same time, corporations "also jumped in, taking advantage of regulators' newly relaxed stock buyback rules"[8]. These corporations bought back securities that the general public had held, thereby making the market for their securities by propping up the price of their securities.

In another case, on March 13, 2008, the Federal Reserve worked out a deal via J. P. Morgan Chase to provide Bear Stearns with a loan against which Bear Stearns pledged as collateral its almost illiquid mortgage backed derivative securities. This permitted Bear Stearns to avoid having to dump their mortgage backed derivative securities on to an already set of failing markets in an attempt to obtain enough liquidity to meet Bear's "repo" loans obligations due on March 14. Accordingly, Bear Stearns gained some breathing room and the selling pressure on financial markets were relieved. J. P. Morgan was the conduit for the loans to Bear Stearns because Morgan had access to the Federal Reserve's discount window and it is also supervised by the Federal Reserve. Bear Stearns did not have access and was not supervised by the Federal

Reserve. Nevertheless, it was obvious on March 13 that if Bear Stearns failed and the collateral insufficient to cover the loan, the Federal Reserve and not J. P. Morgan would take the loss.

On the (Sunday) evening of March 16, the Federal Reserve and J. P. Morgan announced that J. P. Morgan would buy Bear Stearns for the fire sale price of $2 per share. (Bear Stearns shares had closed at $30 per share on Friday March 14.) The Fed also agreed to lend up to $30 billion to J. P. Morgan to finance the illiquid assets it inherits from the purchase of Bear Stearns. In essence the Fed was acting similar to the Resolution Trust Corporation (RTC) that dealt with the illiquid assets of insolvent Savings and Loan banks in the 1989 S&L insolvency crisis[9] by preventing the dumping of financial assets onto the market to obtain cash. The Fed's action saved J. P. Morgan from having to dump Bear Stearns assets on the market to try to obtain enough cash to meet the Bear Stearns obligations.

The post September 11, 2001 activities of the Federal Reserve flooding the banking system directly and other financial institutions with liquidity vividly demonstrates that the central bank can either directly or indirectly "make the market" in financial assets by reducing the outstanding supply of securities available for sale to the general public. The public could then satisfy its increased bearishness tendencies by increasing its money holdings without depressing the market price for financial assets in a disorderly manner. Until, and unless, the public's bearishness recedes, the central bank and the market makers can hold that portion of the outstanding liquid assets that the public does not want to own.

In sum, although the existence of a market maker provides, a higher degree of liquidity for the financial assets, this assurance could dry up in severe sell conditions unless the central bank is willing to take action to provide resources to the private sector market maker or even directly to the market. If the market maker runs down his/her own resources and is not backed by the Monetary Authority central bank indirectly, the asset becomes temporarily illiquid. Nevertheless, the asset holder "knows" that the market maker is providing his/her best effort to search to bolster the buyers' side and thereby restore liquidity to the market.

In markets without a market maker, there can be no assurance that the apparent liquidity of a financial security will not disappear almost instantaneously. Moreover, in the absence of a market maker, there is nothing to inspire confidence that someone is working to try to restore liquidity to the market.

Those who suggest that one only needs a computer-based organization of a market are assuming the computer will always search and find enough participants to buy the security whenever there was a large number of holders who would want to sell. After all, in their theory, the "white noise" variation of buyers' and sellers' offers at prices other than the efficient price in efficient markets is assumed to be normally distributed about the efficient price. Hence, by assumption about the normal symmetrical distribution of buyers and sellers around the price, there can never be a persistent shortage of participants on one side or the other of financial markets.

With the failure of thousands of auction-rate security markets in February 2008, it was obvious that the computers failed to find sufficient buyers. Moreover the computer does not have funds and is not programmed to automatically enter into failing markets and begin purchasing to maintain orderliness when almost everyone wants to sell at, or near, the last market price. The investment bankers who organize and sponsor the securitized markets such as mortgage-backed derivatives, auction rate securities, and other exotic financial assets did not, and would not, act as market makers. These bankers often engaged in "price talk" before the market opened each day[10] to suggest to their clients what they believe the price range of today's market clearing price will likely be. These "price talk" financial institutions, however, did not put their money where their mouth is. They were not required to try to make the market if the actual market price is significantly below their "price talk" estimate.

Nevertheless there are many reports that representatives of these investment bankers had told clients that the holding of these assets "were 'cash equivalents'". Many holders of these exotic securities believed their holdings were very liquid since big financial institutions such as Goldman Sachs, Lehman Brothers, Merrill Lynch, etc. were the dealers who organized the markets and provided the "price talk".

In an article in the February 15/2008 issue of the New York Times it was reported: "Some well-heeled investors got a big jolt from Goldman

Sachs this week; Goldman, the most celebrated bank on Wall Street, refused to let them withdraw money from investments that they considered as safe as cash.... Goldman, Lehman Brothers, Merrill Lynch, etc. have been telling investors the market for these securities is frozen—and so is their cash"[11].

Obviously, up until then, participants in these markets believed they were holding very liquid assets. Nevertheless, the absence of a credible market maker has shown how these assets can easily become illiquid! Had these investors learned the harsh realities of Keynes's liquidity theory, instead of being seduced by the dolce tones of efficient market Sirens, they might never participate in markets whose liquidity could be merely a fleeting mirage. Should not U.S. security laws and regulations provide sufficient information, so investors could have made such an informed decision?

Financial Markets and Regulation Policy

The proper policy response to a financial market crisis similar to what occurred in 2007–2008 can be broken into two parts. First, what can be done to prevent future reoccurrences of this widespread failure of financial markets? Secondly, what, if anything can be done to limit any depressing effects of a credit crunch developed in these securitized financial markets that do not have market makers but the public believed the holdings were "as good as cash".

The question of prevention is the easier of the two to answer.

According to the web page of the United States Securities and Exchange Commission (www.sec.gov): "The mission of the U.S. Securities and Exchange Commission is to protect investors, maintain fair, orderly, and efficient markets, and facilitate capital formation." The SEC web page then goes on to note that the Securities Act of 1933 had two basic objectives: "require that investors receive financial and other significant information concerning securities being offered for public sales, and prohibit deceit, misrepresentations, and other frauds in the sale of securities".

The SEC regulations typically apply to public financial markets where the buyer and the seller of a financial asset do not ordinarily identify themselves to each other. In a public financial market each buyer purchases from the impersonal marketplace and each seller sells to the impersonal market. It is the responsibility of the SEC to assure investors that these public markets are orderly.

In contrast, a private financial market would be where both the buyer and the seller of any financial asset are identified to each other. For example, bank loans are typically a private financial market transaction that would not come under the purview of the SEC. Normally there is no public well organized resale market for securities created in private financial markets. The issued asset from a transaction in a private market traditionally has been an illiquid asset where the lender has "skin in the game" and therefore will not make the loan unless reasonably assured that the borrower will repay the interest due and principle of the debt. And in case of default, the lender hopes the debtor has possession of sufficient collateral as well.

On its web page, The Securities and Exchange Commission also declares that "As more and more first-time investors turn to the markets to help secure their futures, pay for homes, and send children to college, our investor protection mission is more compelling than ever". Given the current experience of contagious failed and failing public financial markets, it would appear that the SEC has been lax in pursuing its stated mission of investor protection. Accordingly the United States Congress should require the SEC to enforce diligently the following rules:

1. *Public notice of potential illiquidity for public markets that do not have a credible market maker.* In the last quarter of a century, large financial underwriters have created public markets, which, via securitization, appeared to convert long term debt instruments (some of them very illiquid, e.g., mortgages) into the virtual equivalent of high yield, very liquid money market funds and other short term deposit accounts. As the newspaper reports that have been cited indicate, given the celebrated status of the investment bank-underwriters of these securities and the statements of their representatives to clients, individual investors were led to believe that they could liquidate their position in the

market that possessed an orderly change in price from the publically announced price of the last public transaction. Moreover the triple AAA rating given by rating agencies such as Standard and Poor to these securitized public market exotic assets added to the belief that these markets would always be very liquid.

This perceived high degree of liquidity for these assets has now proven to be illusionary. Purchasers might have recognized the potential low degree of liquidity associated with these assets if the buyers were informed of all the small print regarding market organization. In markets such as the derivatives markets, for example, although the organizer-underwriter could buy for their own account, they were not obligated to maintain an orderly market. Since the mandate of the SEC is to assure orderly public financial markets, and "require that investors receive financial and other significant information concerning securities being offered for public sales, and prohibit deceit misrepresentations, …. in the sale of securities", it is would seem obvious that all public financial markets that are organized without the existence of a credible market maker should, either (1) be shut down because of the potential for disorderliness, or (2) at a minimum, information regarding the potential illiquidity of such assets should be widely advertised and made part of essential information that must be given to each purchaser of the asset being traded.

The draconian action suggested in (1) above is likely to meet with severe political resistance, as the financial community will argue that in a global economy with the ease of electronic transfer of funds, a prohibition of this sort would merely encourage investors looking for higher yields to deal with foreign financial underwriters and markets to the detriment of domestic financial institutions and domestic industries trying to obtain funding.

In the next chapter we will propose an innovative international payments system[12], that could prevent US residents from trading in foreign financial markets that the U.S. deemed detrimental to American financial firms that obeyed SEC rules while foreign firms did not follow SEC rules. If, however, we assume that the current global payments system remains in effect, and there is a fear of loss of jobs and profits for American firms in the financial industry, then the SEC could permit the existence of public financial markets without a credible market maker as long as the SEC required the organizers of such markets to clearly advertise the possible loss of liquidity that can occur to holders of assets traded in these markets.

A civilized society does not believe in "caveat emptor" for markets where products are sold that can have terribly adverse health effects on the purchaser. Despite the widespread public information that cigarette smoking is a tremendous health hazard, government regulations require cigarette companies to print in bold letters on each package of cigarettes the caution warning that "Smoking can be injurious to your health". In a similar manner, any purchases on an organized public financial market that does not have a credible market maker can have serious financial health effects on the purchasers. Accordingly, the SEC should require the following warning to potential purchasers of assets traded in a market without a credible market maker: *"This market is not organized by a SEC certified credible market maker. Consequently it may not be possible to sustain the liquidity of the assets being traded. Holders must recognize that they may find that their position in these markets can be frozen and they may be unable to liquidate their holdings for cash."*

Furthermore, the SEC should set up strictly enforced rules regarding the minimal amount of financial resources relative to the size of the relevant market that an entity must possess in order to be certified as a credible market maker. The SEC will be required to re-certify all market makers periodically, but at least once a year.

To the extent that mutual fund managers who deal with the public wish to participate in financial markets that operate without a SEC certified credible market maker, then the fund manager must set up a separate mutual fund that only deals in such securities. These specific mutual funds must advertise in bold letters the aforementioned warning – and this warning must be repeated to every investor any time he/she makes an investment in these mutual funds as well as every time the investor receives a statement either electronically or by regular mail of his/her position in the specific mutual fund.

2. *Prohibition against securitization that attempts to create a public market for assets that originated in private markets*—The SEC should prohibit any attempt to create a securitized market for any financial

instrument or a derivative backed by financial instruments that originates in a private financial market (e.g., mortgages, commercial bank loans, auto purchase loans, etc.)

3. *Congress should legislate a 21 century version of the Glass Steagall Act.* The purpose of such an act should force financial institutions to be either an ordinary bank lender creating loans for individual customers in a private financial market, or an underwriter broker who can only deal with instruments created and resold in a public financial market with a credible market maker.

What can be done to mitigate the depressing consequences of another financial crisis that still might develop in the future despite the SEC change in the rules?

There are a number of policy steps that can be taken including (1) the creation of a 21st century equivalents of the Roosevelt era Home Owners Loan Association (HOLC) if the financial crisis is the result of a large wave of defaults in home mortgages, and the George H. W. Bush Administration's Resolution Trust Company (RTC) to alleviate the United States housing bubble crisis and to prevent potential massive insolvency problems, and the (2) the need for massive infusions in cash for financial institutions that are too big to fail.

To a significant extent, the Federal Reserve through its "quantitative easing" [QE] policy has provided a version of providing massive infusions of cash for financial institutions and individuals. QE is an unconventional monetary policy of the central bank when liquidity problems and potential insolvency problems are preventing an economy from responding positively to ordinary monetary policy. QE involves the central bank buying significant amounts of financial assets—not only of government bonds but also often otherwise illiquid financial assets such as derivatives from commercial banks, other private institutions such as pension funds, and even from individuals. This buying of financial assets increases the prices of those financial assets and infuses the selling institutions balance sheets with cash and liquidity, thereby simultaneously increasing the money supply and preventing selling institutions from facing insolvency problems.

In this QE policy, from 2008 till October 2014, the Federal Reserve bought over $3.5 trillion of financial assets including securitized derivatives. The objective was to provide cash to large institutions which had on their balance sheets significant amounts of these financial assets that was losing all market value and becoming a "toxic asset". Without QE by the Federal Reserve the market price of many financial derivatives would have collapse to near zero. Under accepted accounting rules, the financial assets have to be "marked to market". Consequently, the value of the asset side of the balance sheet of these "toxic assets" would collapse reducing or even wiping out most of the net worth of the holders of these securities.

Notes

1. Auction rate securities (ARS) are financial assets backed by long term debts of corporations and/or municipalities where the return paid are reset at frequent intervals through auctions. These auctions provide the primary source of liquidity for holders who want access to cash quickly. In recent years these auctions have failed and consequently holders were unable to liquidate.
2. A credit default swap (CDS) is where the seller will pay the buyer of the CDS if a specified debtor defaults on a specific loan. The buyer need not own the specific debt certificate of the debtor. Consequently CDS are often bought if one wants to bet the debtor will default.
3. If the EMT is buttressed by the assumption of rational expectations, then expectations about the long run assure that short run market prices do not get far out of line with their long run "fundamentals" determined price.
4. L. Summers and V. Summers, "When Financial Markets Work Too Well: A Cautious Case For A Securities Transactions Tax", *Journal of Financial Services, 3*, 1989, p. 166. Emphasis added.
5. Kim, Jane J. and Anand, Shefali, "Some Investors Forced To Hold 'Auction' Bonds: Market Freeze Leaves Them Unable To Cash Out Securities That Were Pitched As 'Safe'" *Wall Street Journal* February 21, 2008, p. D1.
6. Morgenson, Gretchen, (2008),"Arcane Market Is Next To Face Big Credit Test", *New York Times*, February 17, p. A1.

7. Raghavan, Anita, Pulliam, Susan and Opdyke, Jeff, "Team Effort: Banks and Regulators Drew Together To Calm Markets After Attack", *Wall Street Journal*, October 18, 2001, p. A1.
8. Raghavan, Anita, Pulliam, Susan and Opdyke, Jeff, (2001). "Team Effort: Banks and Regulators Drew Together To Calm Markets After Attack", *Wall Street Journal*, October 18, p. A1.
9. The need for a revived Resolution Trust Company to help solve the financial market crisis that was initiated with the sub prime mortgage problem was emphasized in Davidson, P. "How to Solve the U.S. Housing Problem and Avoid Recession: A Revived HOLC and RTC", *Schwartz Center for Economic Policy Analysis: Policy Note*, January 2008, online at: http://eco.bus.utk.edu/davidson.html.
10. Before the day's auction begins, the investment banker will typically provide "price talk" to their clients indicating a range of likely clearing rates for that auction. This range is based on a number of factors including the issuer's credit rating, the last clearance rate for this and similar issues, general macroeconomic conditions, etc.
11. Anderson, Jenny and Bajaj, Vikas. "New Trouble in Auction-Rate Securities", *New York Times*, p. D4, February 15. 2008.
12. The proposed international payments system is a variant of the Keynes Plan that was presented by Keynes at the Bretton Woods conference in 1944 and rejected by the United States.

8

Globalization and International Trade Effects on Employment and Prosperity

Keynes's general theory explains that increases in spending on domestically produced goods and services creates additional profit opportunities for enterprises producing goods in domestic located factories. It follows that the managers of these enterprises would be encouraged to hire additional workers whenever additional profit opportunities exist if more products are produced to sell in the market. In the closed economy model of most textbooks where all market transactions are among residents of the same national economy, it is implicitly assumed that the additional spending would come from domestic households, domestic business firms and/or federal, state or local governments to be spent to purchase the output produced by enterprises located in the domestic economy.

Once the analysis is placed into a globalized market system involving many separate nations things change. For example, spending by United States households, business firms, and even a Federal, state or local US government may go to purchase imports, i.e., goods produced in foreign nations. Domestic spending on imports creates profit and job opportunities in foreign nations and not in the domestic industries economy. On the other hand, demand by foreigners for goods and services produced domestically (i.e., exports) creates profits and jobs for workers in the domestic economy.

If, for example, in any year, exports from nation A equals the imports into nation A, then the foreign profits and job creating effects of nation A's imports will approximately equal the domestic profits job creation opportunities in nation A's export industries. If, however, there is free international trade between nations and nation A imports significantly more than it exports to foreigners, then nation A's spending on imports may, in general, support more profit opportunities and jobs in foreign nations than nation A's export sales creating profit and job opportunities for enterprises located in nation A. Nation A is said to be experiencing an "unfavorable balance of trade". If exports exceed imports, the nation A is experiencing a "favorable balance of trade".

Whenever a nation experiences an unfavorable balance of trade, its imports provide a larger stimulus to foreign economies, then its export sales stimulus to the domestic economy. In 2008, for example, the United States had an unfavorable balance of trade where the US imported $709 billion more goods and services from foreign nations than it exported to foreign markets. This means that foreign nations had a favorable balance of trade with the United States and consequently spent $709 billion less on imports from the Unted States than they earned on their exports to the United States.

Suppose China, Japan, India and other US trading partners who had a favorable balance of trade with US had spent on importing US production of goods their entire 2008 export dollar earnings on sales in US markets instead of not spending (saving) the $709 billion of their earnings from exports to the USA. This hypothetical additional $709 billion spending by these trading partners on United States exports would have been an additional stimulus in 2008 to the US economy equal to approximately 95% of the stimulus that the US federal government authorized in the Obama stimulus spending stimulus bill enacted by the US Congress in 2008 to alleviate the effects of the Great Recession.

Since 1974, the United States has been consistently spending more on imports than it receives in sales revenue from exports, thereby creating more profit opportunities and jobs in foreign nations than foreigners have been creating for the United States in its export industries. The result has been that the United States has acted as the major engine for economic growth for the rest of the world's industries for more than four decades. The impressive economic growth rates displayed by countries like Japan in the 1980s and China and India in the early years of the 21st century owe that prosperity in large part to the United States increases in spending on imports from these nations.

A simple example will illustrate this situation. Let us assume that in any one year the United States spends $10 billion more on Chinese imports (say toys) and therefore $10 billion less on domestically produced toys. Assume that simultaneously China does not increase spending on any United States exports. The US unfavorable balance of trade deficit with China will increase by $10 billion. The effect is that this $10 billion spent by US residents on toy imports from China created profits and jobs in the Chinese toy industry. US residents who diverted their spending on domestically produced toys to foreign produced toys have destroyed potential profit opportunities and jobs in the United States toy industry.

In this hypothetical example, China has "saved" $10 billion out of its international export earnings. Since in the Keynes analysis "a penny saved is a penny that cannot be earned" by anyone else, then in this hypothetical example the $10 billion the Chinese saved is $10 billion that cannot be earned by businesses and workers located in the United States. In discussing the problem of unemployment in the United States, former Federal Reserve chairman Ben Bernanke spoke of this foreign nations' hoarding of dollar earning from exports to the USA as a "glut of savings overseas".

Any nation experiencing an unfavorable balance of trade must finance this trade deficit by either (1) the deficit nation drawing down its previous savings on international earnings (these savings are called the nation's foreign reserves) to pay for its excess of imports over exports, or (2) by the deficit nation borrowing funds from the foreigners in the rest of the world to pay for the difference between the value of imports and the value of exports.

Since the United States imports have exceed exports every year since 1974, the United States, has borrowed from foreigners to finance its excess of imports over exports. The result has been that the United

States has moved from being the world's largest creditor nation to being the largest debtor nation in terms of debt owed to the rest of the world.

To continue with our previous illustrative example, we might ask what do the Chinese do with this $10 billion savings on its international trade earnings? Like all savers the Chinese look for liquid assets to store their international savings which then can be used, in the future, to settle international contractual obligations. The Chinese have used a significant portion of their international savings to purchase United States Treasury securities. This indicates that the Chinese believe the United States dollar is the safest harbor for storing their unused international contractual settlement power savings.

This savings by the Chinese have led many classical theory "experts" to state that the Chinese have been financing the American consumer shopping spree and the resulting growth of United States international debt. These "experts" have warned that if nations such as China stop buying United States securities with their international savings out of international earnings from exports to the United States, then American consumers could no longer afford to buy as many imports and they would have to reduce their purchases of Chinese made goods at retail outlets like Walmart.

The large sums that American consumers spend on imports over the years has generated significant profit and job opportunities for the Chinese. If, for any reason, Americans stopped buying Chinese imports, imagine how this would devastate the profits of Chinese firms and threaten the jobs of Chinese workers. The result could even cause political unrest in China. The Chinese Communist party enjoys popular support as long as it not only protects the nation from foreign enemies but also as long as it continues to support economic actions that result in improvement in employment and living conditions for all Chinese citizens. In other words politically as well as economically it is unlikely to be in China's interest to stop financing Americans' huge Chinese imports over exports to China.

Suppose the Chinese did not use their international savings to buy United States Treasury bonds. Instead, assume, as in our illustrative example, the Chinese spent the $10 billion toy export earnings on the products of American domestically located export industries. The result would be that.

1. China would have more products from American producers. Suppose the Chinese spent more on US agricultural exports such as meat, corn and wheat. If more of these food products were available in China they would strongly embellish and improve the standard food diet of the average Chinese worker.
2. American businesses and their workers would earn more income and therefore the US would not have to borrow from the Chinese to finance their large import purchases of Chinese goods.

The morale of this illustration is that if the Chinese would spend more of their export dollar earnings buying US produced goods instead of buying United States Treasury bonds, then the Chinese government would make available US produced goods to the Chinese population that then would improve Chinese real living standards while more American workers would be employed and would earn enough income to afford all the Chinese imports they are buying but without the US going into debt to the Chinese.

This simple illustration suggests that one engine of growth that a nation such as China might try is to obtain a favorable balance of trade by increasing its exports to the rest of the world. If successful such an export expansion led growth policy will result in increasing profits for enterprises and creating jobs for domestic workers. If, however, any one country runs a favorable balance of trade, then other nation(s) must run an unfavorable balance of trade, resulting in a tendency to lose jobs and profits to the nation pursuing an export led growth policy. Thus, as Keynes noted, if each nation tries to stimulate its economy by running a favorable balance of trade, then this "may lead to a senseless international competition for a favorable balance of trade which injures all alike".[1]

Keynes and his Post Keynesian followers have developed a solution for promoting growth among trading nations while preventing competition among nations to obtain export-led growth via a favorable balance of trade. This solution will end persistent trade imbalances that cause the nation(s) with an unfavorable balance of trade to lose profit and job opportunities while incurring huge international debts. What is required is some form of an institutional arrangement that prevents any persistent trade imbalance among nations by creating an arrangement that induces the creditor nation with the export surplus to spend more on the products of other debtor nations.

In contrast, the classical efficient market theory solution to this persistent trade imbalance problem is to argue that all the pressure should be on the debtor nation to reduce its imports relative to its exports. According to classical theory, one way this can occur is to let the free market determine currency exchanges rates that will end the trade imbalance problem. The classical theory maintains that if the Chinese currency (the renminbi) was traded in a free flexible foreign exchange market without any interference by the Chinese government, and if the United States ran an unfavorable balance of trade with the Chinese, then the demand for the Chinese currency would substantially increase in value relative to the US dollar. As a result, the retail dollar price in the United States of Chinese goods would rise. The resulting rise in the US consumer price level would adversely affect the real income and living standards of the average employed American worker. American consumers would find that Chinese goods were becoming more expensive in terms of dollars and therefore they could no longer afford to buy as much imports from China.

With the appreciation of the Chinese currency relative to the dollar, the Chinese would experience a decline in the renminbi price of United States imports and therefore the Chinese consumer could buy more imports from the United States[2] as their real income and living standard improved. The classical theory assumes that this change in exchange rates will continue until exports equals imports in each country.

If, however, the value of the US dollar declined relative to the Chinese currency, then as the retail dollar price of Chinese imports increases the rate of price inflation in the United States as measured by the consumer price index would rise since imports are a significant portion of the American consumer budget.[3] If the Federal Reserve believes that its primary obligation is to fight a rising price level, then the Federal Reserve's might ramp up its anti-inflationary policy and increase the domestic interest rate. A rise in interest rates in the United States should reduce borrowing to purchase imports and domestic produce goods thereby reducing market demand and profit opportunities for American and Chinese business firms and therefore increase unemployment globally.

But even if we assume the Federal Reserve does not engage in any anti-inflation monetary policy when the dollar price of imports rise because of a change in the exchange rates, the classical exchange rate adjustment answer will tend to reduce global output and employment. In this classical theory scenario, as Americans buy fewer Chinese imports, profits and jobs in China's export industries would be reduced creating some unemployment and potential political unrest in China. With lower incomes in China, the Chinese market demand for United States exports declines resulting in less US profit opportunities than otherwise made possible by the ongoing devaluation of the dollar. Clearly such a possible scenario is neither good for the American or Chinese workers and business firms. The classical solution of the exchange rate change putting pressure on the deficit nation to reduce its import spending will release contractionary forces on the global economic system.

The classical theory avoids this depressing scenario by merely assuming that with free efficient markets there will *always* be full employment of capital and labor in all trading nations no matter what changes occur in the exchange rate of currencies between nations as wage rates in each nation change sufficiently to produce full employment. In other words, classical theory merely assumes away the possible unemployment problem that could occur in both America and China if the free market permits the United States dollar to be devalued relative to the renminbi in order to end the United States' unfavorable balance of trade. In the long run, classical theory asserts as a matter of faith rather than as empirical evidence, there must always be full employment in all nations.[4]

Thus by loading the classical model with sufficient but unrealistic assumptions, classical theory resolves any potential trade deficit problem by merely invoking the magic of free markets for foreign exchange of currencies, in a world where the future is known—at least in the long run.

Some more pragmatic economists have noted that historically when exchange rate have been permitted to change relatively freely in the market the results have often been devastating for a nation. Consequently some experts have advocated a foreign exchange market where a market maker actually fixes the exchange rate at some pre-announced level. As a result, very often economic discussions on the requirements for a good international payments system have been limited to this question of the advantages and disadvantages of fixed vs. flexible exchange rates.

The facts of experience since the end of the Second World War plus Keynes's revolutionary liquidity analysis indicates that more is required than merely deciding whether exchange rates should be fixed or freely flexible. A mechanism must be designed to adequately resolve any persistent trade and international payments imbalances that could occur whether the exchange rates are fixed or flexible. The mechanism should be designed not only to resolve these imbalance problems but also to simultaneously to help promote global full employment—rather than just assume global full employment will always occur. Such a mechanism was embedded in the Bretton Woods Keynes Plan for international trade and payment imbalances.

The Bretton Woods Solution

In 1944, as the Second World War was winding down, the victorious Allied nations organized a conference at Bretton Woods, New Hampshire. The purpose of this Bretton Woods conference was to design a post war international payments system. Keynes was the chief representative of the United Kingdom delegation. In contrast to the classical view of the desirability of free exchange rate markets, Keynes's position was that there is an incompatibility thesis in the classical theory approach to international trade and finance. Keynes argued that permitting free trade, flexible exchange rates and free capital mobility across international borders can be incompatible with the economic goal of global full employment and rapid economic growth.

Keynes offered an alternative analysis to the classical approach to the problem. This alternative was the "Keynes Plan" solution, an arrangement that would make international trade and international financial flow arrangements compatible with global full employment and vigorous global economic growth while, when necessary, permitting nations to introduce controls on any flow of capital funds that was being sent across national boundaries.

Keynes argued that the "main cause of failure" of any traditional international payments system—whether based on fixed or flexible exchange rates—was its inability to actively foster continuous global economic expansion whenever persistent trade payment imbalances occurred among trading nations. This failure, Keynes wrote,

> "can be traced to a single characteristic. I ask close attention to this, because I shall argue that this provides a clue to the nature of any alternative which is to be successful. It is characteristic of a freely convertible international standard that it throws the main burden of adjustment on the country which is in the debtor position on the international balance of payments - that is, on the country which is (in this context) by hypothesis the weaker and above all the smaller in comparison with the other side of the scales which (for this purpose) is the rest of the world."[5]

Keynes concluded that an essential improvement in designing any international payments system requires transferring the major *onus* of adjustment from the debtor to the creditor nation when any persistent international payments imbalance develops. This transfer of responsibility for ending persistent international payment imbalances to those nations that experience exports that exceed their imports and are therefore in the creditor position would, Keynes explained, substitute an expansionist, in place of a contractionist, pressure from world trade. To achieve a golden era of economic development Keynes recommended combining a fixed, but adjustable, exchange rate system with a mechanism for requiring the nation "enjoying" a favorable balance of trade to initiate most of the effort necessary to eliminate this trade imbalance, while "maintaining enough discipline in the debtor countries to prevent them from exploiting the new ease allowed them".[6]

During the Second World War, millions of people had been killed or wounded. Industrial and residential centers in most of Europe lay in ruins. By the end of the war, Europe was on the brink of famine as agricultural production had been disrupted by the war. Transportation infrastructure was in shambles. The war-torn capitalist nations in Europe did not have sufficient undamaged productive resources available to produce enough to feed their populations and much less to rebuild their economies.

The only major economic power in the world that was not significantly damaged by the war was the United States. European rebuilding would require the European nations to run huge import purchases with the United States in order to meet their economic needs for a rebuilding recovery. At the same time these European nations did not possess undamaged production facilities to produce goods to sell to the US in order to earn dollars to buy US exports. The European nations also had very little foreign reserves so they could not draw down these reserves sufficiently to buy American exports. (At the time the major foreign reserves were in the form of the asset gold).

The only alternative, under a free market *laissez-faire* system, would be for Europeans to obtain an enormous volume of dollar loans from the private sector of the United States to finance the purchase of United States exports needed to feed the European population and rebuild their economies. Private sector lenders in the United States, however, were mindful that German reparation payments to the victorious Allied nations after the First World War were primarily financed by American private investors lending to Germany (the so-called Dawes Plan). Germany never repaid these Dawes plan loans. Given this history of a nation defaulting on international debt repayments after a major war and the existing circumstances immediately after the Second World War, it was obvious that private lending facilities in the United States could not be expected to provide the loans necessary for European recovery.

The Keynes Plan, presented at the 1944 Bretton Woods conference, would require the United States, as the obvious major creditor nation, to accept the major responsibility for curing the post war trade imbalance where a tremendous amount of goods from the United States would be necessary to feed the populations in Europe while simultaneously rebuilding the factories and infrastructure necessary to reestablish viable productive European economies.

Where were the Europeans going to get the finance to purchase all the necessary goods from the United States? Keynes estimated that the European nations might require in excess of $10 billion to purchase United States exports for such a post-war rebuilding of the European economies. The Keynes Plan had an operational system that would have the United States simply provide these funds to the Europeans. The United States representative to the Bretton Woods Conference, Harry Dexter White, stated that the US Congress would never provide the $10 billion that Keynes estimated was the minimum required funding. Instead, White argued, the United States Congress might be willing to provide, at most, $3 billion as the United States contribution to solving this post war international financial problem for rebuilding European economies.

The United States delegation at the Bretton Woods conference was the most important participant. It was clear that nothing could be done unless the United States delegation agreed to any plan that was developed at the conference. White had the US delegation veto the Keynes Plan. Instead, White provided a plan that set up the International Monetary Fund (IMF) and what we now call the World Bank.

The White plan envisioned the International Monetary Fund (IMF) providing short-term loans to nations running unfavorable balances of trade. These loans were supposed to give the debtor nation time to rebuild its economic structure and then stop importing more than it was exporting. Then these debtor nations were to pay off their debt to the IMF by earnings from their exports exceeding their import purchases. Under the White Plan, the United States would subscribe a maximum of $3 billion as its contribution to the IMF lending facilities.

The World Bank would borrow funds from the free market. These World Bank funds would then be used to provide long-term loans for rebuilding capital facilities and making capital improvements initially in the war-torn nations and later in the less developed countries. When the new facilities were in place, it was assumed that sufficiently more goods could be produced and sold profitably. Then the nation would use the new income earned from the new facilities to pay off the World Bank loans. This White plan suggested by the US delegation was basically the institutional arrangements adopted at the Bretton Woods Conference.

Under this White plan, international loans from the IMF or the World Bank were the only available sources for financing the huge volume of imports from the United States that the war-torn nations would require *immediately* after the Second World War. It turned out, however, that the IMF and World Bank together did not have sufficient funds to make loans of the magnitude needed by the European nations. But even if the IMF and the World Bank could have provided loans sufficient to meet the needs of the war torn nations, the result would have been a huge international indebtedness of these nations. Paying off this immense debt obligations would require the European population to accept the main burden of adjustment by them being willing to "tighten their belts" (In the 21 century international lexicon, the debtor nation should adopt a strict "austerity" program).

This belt tightening statement is a euphemism to indicate that the debtor nations would have to dramatically reduce their consumption spending for imports and even goods produced domestically. Such a plan could be put into effect only by reducing the income of the residents of European nations so they only can afford to buy less output from both foreign and domestic enterprises, while the nation is simultaneously paying the annual debt servicing charges. This implied no significant improvement in the standard of living of Europeans for years to come. The result would so depress Europeans as to possibly inducing political revolutions in most of Western Europe. Not inconsequentially, the tighten your belt policies also would have limited Europe as a possible large profitable market in the future for American exporters.

To avoid the possibility of many European nations facing a desperate electorate that might opt for a communist system when faced with the dismal future the White Plan offered, the United States developed an alternative plan in the hope that Communism did not spread west from the Soviet Union to the democratic European nations. In 1948, President Truman recommended Congress accept the Marshall Plan. Despite White's argument that the United States would not be willing to give more than $3 billion to solving this international payments problem, the Congress approved the Marshall Plan which provided $5 billion in foreign aid in 18 months and a total of $13 billion in four years. (Adjusted for inflation, this $13 billion sum is equivalent to approximately $170 billion in 2017 dollars). The Marshall plan was essentially a four year *gift* of $13 billion worth of American exports to the war devastated nations. The Marshall Plan required no repayment by the recipients of these funds—and hence no "belt tightening".

The 1948 Marshall plan gifts gave the recipient nations a sufficient number of dollars to buy approximately 2% of the total annual output (Gross Domestic Product) of the United States each year for four years. Despite Americans giving away 2% of their national income per annum, there was no real sacrifice for American households associated with the Marshall Plan as the remaining income was significantly greater than pre-war levels. The United States standard of living during the first year of the Marshall Plan was still 25% larger than it had been in the last peacetime year of 1940. American household income continued to grow throughout the Marshall Plan period.

The Marshall Plan funds created profit opportunities for American firms and jobs for US workers. Full employment was readily sustained. Immediately after the war ended, US government military spending was significantly reduced, which by itself might have created a post-war unemployment problems. Offsetting this reduction in government military spending was the Marshall plan funds spending that created significant increases in employment in United States export industries just as several million men and women were discharged from the United States armed forces and entered the United States civilian labor force looking for jobs.

For the first time in its history, the United States did not suffer from a severe recession due to a lack of spending immediately following the cessation of a major war and a reduction in military spending by the federal government. The United States and most of the rest of the world experienced an economic "free lunch" as both the potential debtor nations and the creditor nation experienced tremendous real economic gains resulting from the Marshall Plan and other foreign aid give aways. Despite the growth in output from foreign factories, however, the United States maintained a surplus merchandise trade balance of exports over imports until the first oil price shock in 1973.

By 1958, however, although the United States still had an annual goods and services export surplus of over $5 billion, the post war United States potential international payments surplus was at an end. By that time United States governmental foreign and military aid to allied nations exceeded $6 billion. There was also a net private capital outflow of $1.6 billion from the United State that financed United States companies investing in productive facilities abroad. This total of $7.6 outflow of funds more than offset the earnings of the $5 billion export surplus by $2.6 billion. In other words by 1958, the international payments account of the United States saw a net outflow of $2.6 billion despite export earnings exceeding spending on imports by $5 billion. The post war United States international payments surplus was at an end.

As the United States total international payments account swung into deficit in 1958 other nations began to experience international payments surpluses. These credit surplus nations did not spend their payments surpluses on additional imports from the United States. Instead the nations used their unspent annual dollar surpluses to purchase the international liquid asset which at that time was the gold reserves of the United States. For example, in 1958, the United States sold over $2 billion in gold reserves to foreign central banks.

These trends accelerated in the 1960s, partly as a result of increased United States military and financial aid in response to the construction of the Berlin Wall in 1961 and later because of the US's increasing military involvement in Vietnam. At the same time, a rebuilt Europe and Japan became important producers of exports so that the rest of the world became less dependent on purchasing export products solely from United States industries.

Still the United States maintained a surplus merchandise trade balance of exports over imports until the first oil price shock in 1973. More than offsetting this trade surplus during most of the 1960s, however, were foreign and military aid dollar outflows to other nations plus net capital outflows from the United States that financed United States companies investing in facilities abroad. Consequently during the 1960's years the United States experienced an annual unfavorable total balance of international payments.

The Bretton Woods system had no way of automatically forcing the emerging creditor nations experiencing an international payments surplus to step up and accept the responsibility for resolving the persistent payments imbalances—a creditor adjustment role that contributed so wonderfully to post Second World War global economic growth. A creditor role that the United States had started playing in 1948 with the Marshall Plan. Instead during the 1960s the surplus nations continued to convert some portion of their annual dollar international payment receipt surpluses into demands on United States gold reserves to be stored as a liquid asset for savings that could be used anytime in the future to meet international payments obligations. As surplus nations in the 1960s drained gold reserves from the United States, the seeds of the destruction of the Bretton Woods system and the golden age of global economic development were being sown.

In 1971, President Richard Nixon closed the gold window. Nixon stated that the United States government would no longer sell gold to foreign nations who had earned dollars and wanted to use these dollars to buy gold from the United States rather than buy produced goods and services from American business firms. Nixon's closing of the gold window had, in essence, indicated that the United States was unilaterally withdrawn from any Bretton Woods agreement. At that point of time, the last vestiges of Keynes's enlightened international monetary approach where the creditor nation accepts a large responsibility for correcting persistent international payments imbalances was on its way to be forgotten.

Reforming the International Payments System

The post Second World War global golden age of economic development required international institutions and United States government foreign aid policies that operated on principles inherent in the Keynes Plan where the creditor nation accepting the major responsibility for solving any persistent international payments imbalance. The formal Breton Woods agreement, however, did not require creditor nations to take such actions. Since Nixon's closing of the gold window in 1971, the onus has been on nations with deficits in their trade and international payments balances to solve their own international deficit payments problems—usually through some policy of austerity. The result has been that since 1971 the international payments system often impedes rapid economic growth and even induces contractionary forces on many nations of the world.

Utilizing the ideas Keynes presented at Bretton Woods, it is possible to update the Keynes Plan for a 21st century international monetary payments scheme that would eliminate persistent unfavorable payments imbalances, promote global economic prosperity and still meet the political realities of today without bowing one's knee to efficient market advocates. For, as Keynes wrote:

> "to suppose [as the classical theory does] that there exists some smoothly functioning automatic [free market] mechanism of adjustment which preserves equilibrium if only we trust to methods of laissez-faire is a doctrinaire delusion which disregards the lessons of historical experience without having behind it the support of sound theory."[7]

Since the 1990s, there has been several international finance crises. In 1994 when the Mexican government was faced with difficulties in trying to service its international debt repayments, some pragmatic policy makers recognized that free markets do not provide a system that automatically prevents a crisis in the international payments sector. In some cases, instead of relying on the market to solve the problem, these pragmatists advocated the creation of some sort of *crisis manager* to stop international financial market liquidity hemorrhaging and to "bail-out" the international investors. In 1994, United States Treasury Secretary Robert Rubin encouraged President Clinton to use American funds to lend to Mexico to solve its financial crisis and thereby save the wealth of international buyers of Mexican bonds. This solved the problem.

In other cases, when the solution was left to the free market severe economic problems developed. In 1997, for example, Thailand, Malaysia, and other East Asian nations experienced an international currency crisis that battered their economies. In 1998 the Russian debt default caused another international financial crisis that lead to the collapse of the Long Term Capital Management (LTCM) hedge fund which, except for quick action by pragmatists at the New York Federal Reserve Bank, could have induced a significant drop in American equity markets. (We should note that among the principals of LTCM was Nobel Prize economist winner Myron Scholes, who won his Nobel Prize for discovering the formula for free market "properly" pricing risk in an efficient financial market environment. Scholes formula, however, could not save LTCM from its after-the-fact recognized investment blunder into Russian bonds by not correctly pricing the risks involved in such an investment).

At the time of the Russian debt default and the LTCM collapse, President Clinton called for a "new financial architecture" for international financial market transactions. The then International Monetary Fund Director Stanley Fischer (who in 2014 Obama appointed as Vice Chair of the Federal Reserve) recognized that the IMF did not have sufficient funds to stem the international financial crises that was occurring. Fisher suggested that the major nations of the world, the so called G-7 nations, make a temporary arrangement where they would provide additional financing to help provide funds to any nation suffering from deficits in its international payments imbalances until such nations could get their economic house in order.

Fisher's cry for a G-7 temporary collaboration to provide funds to deficit nations is equivalent to recruiting a volunteer fire department to douse the flames after someone has cried fire in a crowded theater. Even if the fire is ultimately extinguished there will be a lot of innocent casualties. Moreover, every new currency fire would require the G-7 voluntary fire department to pour more liquidity into the market to put out the flames. Clearly a more desirable goal would be to produce a permanent fire prevention system, and not to rely on organizing larger and larger volunteer fire fighting companies with each new currency crisis. In other words, crisis prevention rather than crisis management should be the policy goal.

President Clinton's clarion call for a new international financial architecture implicitly recognized the need for a permanent prevention institutional arrangement in the existing international payments system. Unfortunately, President Clinton's call was not taken up as the international community managed to muddle through the experience although some nations and its residents suffered severe economic pains.

Beginning in 2007 the global economic system again experienced a global financial crisis—a crisis of much larger proportions than those in the 1990s. The US subprime mortgage derivatives problem created a contagious disease that caused havoc with banking systems in many other countries including Germany, the United Kingdom, France, Spain, Greece and others. The contagion caused the almost complete collapse of the Icelandic banking system and even the Swiss banking system—usually considered a paragon of financial stability—appeared for a while to be in severe economic trouble. The need for a "new international financial architecture" is clearly more urgent than ever.

In the 21st century interdependent global economy, a substantial degree of economic cooperation among trading nations is essential. The original Keynes Plan for reforming the international payments system called for the creation of a single Supranational Central Bank. Given the problems the European Union has suffered despite it possessing a Supranational European central bank suggests that perhaps an institutional arrangement that avoids such a Supranational central bank may be more desirable in that it permits participating nations to still manage their own monetary policy in the way the government thinks is in the best interests of its residents.

Reforming the International Payments System

An international financial architecture system to deal with persistent trade imbalances and any international financial crisis can be developed to operate under the same economic principles laid down by Keynes at Bretton Woods. But this system does not require the establishment of a supranational central bank of the world as Keynes suggested in his "Keynes Plan" at Bretton Woods. Instead, this new international payment system is aimed at obtaining a more acceptable international agreement (given today's political climate in most nations) that does not require any nation to surrender the nation's control of either its domestic banking system or the operation of its domestic monetary and fiscal policies to a supranational authority. Each nation will still be able to use monetary and fiscal policies to determine the domestic economic destiny that is best for its citizens as long as it does not detrimentally affect employment and income earning opportunities in other trading partner nations.

What is required is a closed, double-entry bookkeeping clearing institution to keep the international payments 'score' among the various trading nations plus some mutually agreed upon rules enforced by the clearing institution to solve the problems of persistent trade and international payment imbalances. It will also require an international agreement and a method to prevent international financial market transactions that can cause a financial market crisis that would be disruptive to the stability of any nation's economy as well as a threat to the global economy.

The new international institution to be set up under this plan could be labeled the International Monetary Clearing Union (IMCU). The IMCU would require all international payments between nations whether for imports or financial funds crossing national borders to go through this International Monetary Clearing Union. Each nation's central bank will set up a deposit account with the IMCU. Then any payments of a resident entity in nation A made to a resident entity in nation B will have to clear through each nation central bank deposit at the IMCU. A payment from a resident in nation A to a resident in nation B when cleared through the IMCU would appear as a credit for nation's B central bank account at the IMCU and as debit to nation's A central bank's account at the IMCU. Although this may seem to be a complicated process to the average layperson, it is merely an international version of how checks are cleared when a resident of one region of the United States, say California, pays other entities in another region, say New York. These checks clear thru the clearing house mechanism set up by the United States Federal Reserve System.

This IMCU is a 21st century variant of the Keynes Plan. To operate it would require several technical properties to assure it can enforce rules that deal with all types of international financial problems [These technical requirements are spelled out in more detail in my book *Post Keynesian Theory and Policy*]. At this point, rather than letting the exposition getting bogged down in some technical details it is more appropriate to indicate how this IMCU proposal works to end the possibility of persistent trade imbalances and disruptive flows of financial funds across national borders. Simultaneously this IMCU would be encouraging global full employment and economic growth.

The object of this International Monetary Clearing Union is

1. to prevent a lack of global effective market demand for the products of industry occurring due to international liquidity problems occurring whenever any nation(s) holds either excessive idle foreign reserves in its deposit account at the IMCU. The IMCU would have the power to encourage sufficient spending globally to produce enough profit incentives in export industries of nations to help assure global full employment,
2. to provide an automatic mechanism for placing a major burden of correcting international trade and payments imbalances on the nation running persistent payments surpluses,
3. to provide each nation with the ability to monitor and, if desired, to control international cross border movements (a) of flight financial funds, as well as money moved across national borders in order to avoid paying taxes on such funds, and (b) of earnings from illegal activities leaving the nation, and (c) to prevent funds that cross borders to finance terrorist operations,
4. to expand the quantity of the IMCU liquid international financial asset used in settling international contracts commitments as global capacity warrants while protecting the international purchasing power of this IMCU asset.

The IMCU system would have a built-in mechanism to encourage any nation that runs persistent trade surpluses of exports over imports to spend what is deemed (in advance) by agreement of the international community to be "excessive" credit balances (savings) of foreign liquid reserve assets that have been deposited in the nation's central bank's deposit account at the IMCU. These accumulated credits (saving out of international earned income) represent funds that the creditor nation could have used to buy the products of foreign industries but instead used to increase its foreign reserves in terms of its deposit at the IMCU. When a nation holds excessive credits in its deposit account at the IMCU, it would mean that these excess credits are creating significant unemployment problems and the lack of profitable opportunities for business enterprises somewhere in the global economy.

The Keynes principle involved in this situation is to recognize that if the creditor nation spends internationally its excessive credits, this spending will increase profit opportunities and the hiring of workers around the globe and thereby promote global full employment. It will also provide the opportunity for borrowers around the world to potentially earn more income that can be used to service any international debt obligations that they may owe.

The Keynes solution would encourage the creditor nation to spend these excessive credits at the IMCU in three possible ways—all beneficial to the global economy. These three ways are:

1. On the products (exports) of any other deficit member nation of the IMCU.
2. On new direct foreign investment projects in other IMCU member nations, and/or.
3. To provide foreign aid, similar to the Marshall Plan, to deficit IMCU members.

The credit nation is free to choose any combination of the above three ways to spend its excessive credit at the IMCU but it must spend its excessive credits to help the deficit nation.

If the creditor nation spends its excessive credits on imports from foreign producers, the result will be that the surplus nation's trade imbalance will be reduced while it is creating additional profits opportunities and labor hiring in other nations. This means more income for people and businesses in the nations previously experiencing unfavorable balances of trade and who were depleting the deposit at the IMCU and/or borrowing from foreigners to buy their excess of imports over exports. In essence this excess credit IMCU deposit spending on imports gives the deficit nations the opportunity to work their way out of international debt by earning additional income by selling additional exports to their creditors. Certainly this is a more preferable solution than requiring the deficit nations to adopt an "austerity" program which will reduce its purchases of imports such as that advocated by some European Union nations on debtor countries such as Greece.

Direct foreign investment spending requires the nation with excess credits in its IMCU account to build plant and equipment in the deficit nation, thereby immediately increasing profits, jobs and income in the construction industries in the deficit nation and then creating jobs opportunities in manning the new plant and equipment when construction is completed. If the nation receiving this direct foreign investment is a less developed country, then this foreign direct investment spending helps to build the facilities of this less developed country up to 21st century standards.

Foreign aid spending provides the deficit nation with a "gift" that it can use to reduce its debt obligations and/or buy additional products from foreign producers without going further into debt.

These three spending alternatives encourage the surplus nation to accept a major responsibility for correcting trade and international payments imbalances. Nevertheless this provision gives the trade surplus creditor country considerable discretion in deciding how to accept the onus of adjustment in the way it believes is in its residents best interests. It does not permit, however, the surplus nation to shift the burden to the deficit nation(s) by lending the deficit nation or nations more and therefore imposing on any deficit nation additional contractual debt repayments obligations independent of what the deficit nation can afford to repay.

The important thing is to make sure that continual over saving by the surplus nation in the form of international liquid reserves are not permitted to unleash contractionary economic forces on other nations and/or to build up of international debts so encumbering as to impoverish the global economy of the 21 century.

In the event that the surplus nation does not spend or give away the credits that are deemed "excessive" within a specified time, then the IMCU managers would confiscate (and redistribute to debtor members) the portion of credits deemed excessive. This last resort is the equivalent of a 100% taxes on a nation's excessive liquidity holdings that the international community has already agreed are excessive. Since continual excessive liquidity holdings implies continuing and excessive unemployment in one or more nations running trade deficits, if the surplus nation does not spend its excessive surplus, then confiscating these excessive credits and providing them to debtor nations will not only benefit the debtors but improve the global employment rate and output. Of course the nation with excessive credits will recognize that these credits are subject to a 100% tax if not spent. It is therefore highly unlikely that this confiscatory tax will ever have to be enforced.

Under either a fixed or a flexible rate system with each nation free to decide how much it will import, some nations will, at times, experience persistent trade deficits merely because their trading partners are not living up to their means—that is because other nations are continually saving (hoarding) a portion of their foreign export earnings in its IMCU deposit rather than spending it on the products of foreign workers and enterprises. By so doing, these over savers are creating a lack of global market demand for the products that global industries can produce.

Under the Keynes principle requiring creditor nations to spend excessive credits, deficit countries would no longer have to tighten their belts and to install austerity measures reducing the income of their residents in an attempt to reduce imports and thereby reduce their payment imbalance because others are excessively over saving. Instead, the system would seek to remedy the payment deficit by increasing opportunities for deficit nations to sell more products profitably abroad thereby earning more income and thus work their way out of their otherwise deteriorating debtor position.

As the 2007–2008 global financial crisis deepened, some recognized that merely attempting to tinker with the existing system by perhaps upgrading the power of the International Monetary Fund and the World Bank or encouraging the G-7 to again act as a volunteer fire department did not solve the international trade and financial payments problems. For years now the international system has been running into trouble while patches to the existing IMF and World Bank system were applied in a vain attempt to end these global trade and payments problems. The world lost a great opportunity in 1944 when the United

States vetoed the Keynes Plan at Bretton Woods. Let us hope we do not squander this opportunity again.

When the 2009 Obama stimulus recovery spending plan took effect, whatever economic recovery that the American economy experienced again placed the United States as the engine of growth for China and many other less developed nations. It tend to aggravate the United States international payments imbalance problem as, after 2009, the United States began again to increase its imports by a greater amount than its increasing volume of exports. If this result continues, then, under the existing international payments system, the result may be to create an atmosphere where many fear the status of the dollar as the most liquid safe harbor foreign reserve asset. Such fears can only roil global financial markets and plunge the global economy into further crisis and recession.

If this were to occur, it should be even more obvious that a reform of the international trade and payments system is necessary if we are not to further aggravate any global economic crisis. Hopefully, the leaders of the major nations will recognize the need to adopt some form of the Keynes Plan such as the IMCU if the global economy is ever to reinstate prosperous times for all the nations on earth.

The Case for Capital Controls

Since the future is uncertain, at any moment of time some event (ephemeral or not) may occur which can make residents of a nation feel more uncertain about the prospects of their economy. Under a system of free exchange markets, residents of the nation that fear the future can remove their savings from the domestic banking system and transfer them to another nation's banking and financial system where they believe the latter is a safer harbor to store their savings. The funds used in any attempt to find a safe haven in another nation is called "flight capital". If enough people try at the same time to move their funds from the domestic economy to this presumed safe harbor, the effect is similar to a run on a domestic bank that causes the bank to collapse.

In the case of bank runs, a policy of insuring deposits is usually sufficient to stopping bank runs. Unfortunately, a cascade of flight capital fund movements out of a nation to a safe harbor in another nation cannot be stopped by merely insuring the deposits at domestic banks. Instead this flight of funds if large enough can bring about the collapse of the domestic economy, as more and more people stop buying domestically produced goods to increase their holdings of foreign liquid assets. This creates significant recessionary pressures on the domestic economy thereby making it more difficult for the government to undertake economic policies to stabilize the nation's economy and prevent it from falling into recession or depression.

Since under the IMCU proposal all movement of funds across borders must go through the nation's central bank deposit at the IMCU, any nation can, if it desires, monitor and stop any cross border financial fund movements by merely refusing to allow the cross border banking transactions to be processed through the central bank's deposit on the IMCU's books. In other words each nation can institute an effective policy to limit fund outflows from its country if, for any reason, the government deems it in the best interest of the nation's economy to prevent such fund outflows.

If such a system was in place, the United States government could stop flight capital funds outflows when, for example, a Security Exchange Commission ruling prohibits sales of securities—such as mortgage backed derivatives—that are organized by investment bankers but do not have a reliable market maker institution to insure orderliness and liquidity. Under this capital control provision, the American financial services industries would not have to fear loss of customers and profits to foreign financial services firms who do not follow SEC rules when the SEC prohibited certain financial market activities by American financial services firms. The flow of funds could occur only if the foreign financial service firms agreed to all the SEC rules required of domestic financial service firms. Thus the playing field would be level.

Finally, all movements of funds gained from illegal activities, or funds being moved from a country to another nation in order to avoid the domestic country's tax collector, or funds raised in one country that is being funneled to other countries to finance international terrorist activities must flow through the nation's central bank to the IMCU. Consequently, each nation has the facility, if it wishes to monitor and if necessary stop such cross border money flow transactions from occurring. Clearly this is an important aspect of the IMCU plan for it permits each nation to assure its citizens that others cannot take advantage of the international trading system to avoid paying one's fair share of taxes, and to constrain the international financing of terrorist organizations, as well as to permit the government to undermine the profitability of any international illegal drug trade.

The Rules of the IMCU

Only central banks can hold deposits at the IMCU. Each central bank will set its own rules regarding making available foreign monies (through IMCU clearing transactions) to its own bankers and private sector residents[8] who need foreign money to settle legal international contracts denominated in terms of a foreign currency.

Each nation's central bank must agree to sell their own currency (one-way convertibility) against the IMCU at a specified exchange rate per IMCU deposit unit only to other nations' central bank. Each nation agrees that they hold only IMCU deposits as liquid reserve assets for international financial transactions. Accordingly, there can be no draining of reserves from the international payments system. All major private international transactions must clear between central banks' accounts in the books of the international clearing institution.

The exchange rate between the domestic currency of a nation and the IMCU is set initially by each nation or currency union's central bank—just as it would be if one instituted an international gold standard. Since private enterprises that are already engaged in trade have international contractual commitments that would span the changeover interval from the current system, then, as a practical matter, one would expect, but not demand, that the existing exchange rate structure (with perhaps minor modifications) would provide the basis for initial exchange rate setting.

A system to stabilize the long-term purchasing power of the IMCU in terms of each member nation's domestically produced market basket of goods) can be developed. This requires a system of fixed exchange rates between each nation's local currency and the IMCU that changes only to reflect inflation in the price level of domestically produced goods. If, for example, a foreign nation permits wage-price inflation to occur within its borders, then, the exchange rate between the local currency and the IMCU will be devalued to reflect the inflation in the local money price of the domestic produced goods and services. For example, if this rate of domestic inflation was 5%, the exchange rate would change so that each unit of IMCU could purchase 5% more of the nation's currency. By devaluing the exchange rate between local monies and the IMCU to offset the rate of domestic inflation, the IMCU's purchasing power is stabilized and inflation in one nation cannot be exported to another via the price of the first nation's exports.

By restricting use of IMCUs to Central Banks, private speculation regarding IMCUs as a hedge against inflation is avoided. Each nation's rate of inflation of the goods and services it produces is determined solely by (a) the local government's policy toward the level of domestic money wages and profit margins vis-a-vis productivity gains. Each nation is therefore free to experiment with policies for preventing inflation as long as these policies do not lead to a lack of global effective demand. Whether the nation is successful or not in preventing domestic goods price inflation, the IMCU will never lose its international purchasing power in terms of any domestic money.

A trigger mechanism to encourage any creditor nation to spend what is deemed (in advance) by agreement of the international community to be "excessive" credit balances in its IMCU account. These excessive credits can be spent in three ways: (a) on the products of any other member of the clearing union, (b) on new direct foreign investment projects, and/or (c) to provide unilateral transfers (foreign aid) to deficit members.

In the unlikely event that the surplus nation does not spend or give away these credits within a specified time, then the clearing agency would confiscate (and redistribute to debtor members) the portion of credits deemed excessive.[9] This last resort confiscatory action (a 100%

taxes on excessive liquidity holdings) would make a payments adjustment via unilateral transfer payments in the current accounts.

Notes

1. J. M. Keynes, The General Theory of Employment, interest and Money (London, Macmillan, 1936) pp. 338–339.
2. For technical reasons (known as when the Marshall-Lerner conditions are not applicable) that we need not discuss here, it is possible that even with a decline in the value of the United States dollar relative to the Chinese currency, the value of the trade imbalance between China and the United States would not disappear and—in the worse case scenario—the trade imbalance between China and the United States could actually worsen. We will ignore this possible real world complication in the following discussion to illustrate other possible deleterious effects of this classical theory solution to trade imbalances where free markets are suppose always to solve any trade imbalance problem by devaluing the currency of the country experiencing an unfavorable balance of trade.
3. If money wages of American workers did not increase, then the result of this classical theory solution would be to lower the standard of living of the average American worker until it approached the standard of living of Chinese workers.
4. And as endnote#2 indicates, mainstream economists assume always all possible economic problems.
5. J. M. Keynes, The Collected Writings of John Maynard Keynes, 25, edited by D. Moggridge, (Macmillan, London, 1980) p. 27.
6. Op. Cit., p. 176.
7. J. M. Keynes (1941), "Post War Currency Policy" printed in The Collected Writings of John Maynard Keynes, 25, edited by D. Moggridge (Macmillan, London, 1980) pp. 21–22.
8. Correspondent banking will have to operate through the International Clearing Agency, with each central bank regulating the international relations and operations of its domestic banking firms. Small scale smuggling of currency across borders, etc., can never be completely eliminated. But such movement's are merely a flea on a dog's back—a minor, but not debilitating, irritation. If, however, most of the residents of a nation hold and use (in violation of legal tender laws) a foreign currency

for domestic transactions and as a store of value, this is evidence of a lack of confidence in the government and its monetary authority. Unless confidence is restored, all attempts to restore economic prosperity will fail.
9. Whatever "excessive" credit balances that are redistributed shall be apportioned among the debtor nations (perhaps based on a formula which is inversely related to each debtor's per capita income and directly related to the size of its international debt) to be used to reduce debit balances at the clearing union.

9

Are Free Trade Agreements Always Beneficial?

One of the most widely believed policy conclusions of classical economic theory is that free trade among nations is beneficial to all trading nations since free trade always provides more goods and services for residents in all of the free trade nations while fully employing all the productive resources of each trading nation. Accordingly, classical theory indicates that all import and export markets should be made permanently free of any government regulations and/or restrictions such as tariffs or quotas. The conclusion of classical theory is that nations such as the United States will be better off if it would pursue free trade agreements with all other nations on the globe. What is the classical theory basis for such a conclusion?

The classical theory analysis produced a "law of comparative advantage" which it is claimed is a universal applicable truth that assures free trade produces more goods and services globally with resources in every nation fully employed in their most comparative cost (supply side) productive capacity. Each nation will specialize in producing and exporting products from those domestic industries that have a "comparative advantage" in costs of production.

Comparative advantage of a nation's industry is determined by supply side relationships regarding the productivity of capital and labor in the specific production process used to produce goods and services. In each trading nation any government interference with a free trading relationship between nations following the law of comparative advantage, classical theory claims, will reduce the economic prosperity of the nations involved from reaching their potential optimal production output given its supply of capital and labor.

Adam Smith,[1] however, had a different reason for advocating trade between nations. Smith believed that the ability of any nation to produce additional income and wealth is constrained primarily by the extent of demand in the marketplace and not supply side comparative cost limitation conditions. By expanding the market for goods, Smith argued, the introduction of trade between nations permitted entrepreneurs in each nation to take advantages of the production economies of scale in their industry, thereby producing more from each additional worker employed and thereby enhancing the income and the wealth of the nation.

For Adam Smith growth in economic activity was primarily demand driven. The key is the expansion of market demand. An obvious moral of Smith's analysis is that no nation that aspires to be wealthy can be an island unto itself. Instead it must expand production via export market demand for the products of an industry that has economies of scale.

Implicit in the Smith analogy is that consumers in the domestic market for the products of domestic industries are already satiated with the goods and services produced so that domestic market expansion for domestic produced goods to take advantage of the economies of scale is not possible. In any case, supply cost constraints has no significant role to play in Smith's inquiry into what limits the wealth of nations at any point of time.

In 1819 the classical economist David Ricardo developed the concept of the law of comparative advantage to justify the importance of free trade among nations. Since Ricardo, advocates of international free trade have invoked the need for each nation to specialize in the domestic industry (industries) that has a comparative cost advantage in order to increase income and wealth in the face of supply constraints. Unlike

Smith's argument, this Ricardian need for industry specialization of each trading nation to increase the wealth of nations does not rely on expanding market demand to be able to capture the economies of scale in domestic production. In a Ricardian world of trade, production in each nation occurs in the realm of diminishing returns where, as we have explained in our earlier chapter, the additional volume of goods produced by hiring an additional worker in a domestic industry is less than the addition to output produced by the previously last worker hired so that costs of production rise with expansion. In Ricardo's scheme increases in aggregate domestic market demand will not, *per se*, lead to a significant increase in the growth of the wealth of nations, especially in the face of diminishing returns which results in rising production costs per additional unit of output.

Rather, an increase in the wealth of trading nations depends on the law of comparative advantage determining the geographical location of industries based on supply side relative real costs of production and the resulting trade patterns between nations. These real costs are measured in terms of the amount of labor time it takes to produce a unit of output.

To explain this classical law of comparative advantage, assume there are two nations A and B and two industries #1 and #2 and both nations, before trade, are producing products from both industry #1 and industry #2. The law of comparative advantage states that Nation A should specialize solely in production in that industry (industry #1) for which it has the greatest production cost advantage compared to production costs of the same industries #1 and #2 located in nation B. The law then states that Nation B should specialize only in production from industry #2 where it may have a cost advantage, or at least a lesser cost disadvantage relative to industries in Nation A. This result of Nation A's specialization entirely in industry #1 production should occur even if Nation A also has an absolute production cost advantage in industry #2 relative to the costs of industry #2 in Nation B.

In other words even if Nation A has an absolute cost advantage in both industries compare to the costs of these industries in Nation B, if Nation B has a comparatively smaller cost disadvantage in industry #2 than its cost disadvantage in industry #1 compared to industries in nation A, then Nation A should concentrate its resources on production in industry #1, producing all that domestic market demands and exporting to Nation B all the product of industry #1 that the residents of Nation B demand in the market. Nation B should concentrate its resources on production in industry #2—where it the smaller cost disadvantage—to meet all Nation B's domestic demand plus export demand to Nation A of r the product of industry #2. The resulting geographical industry pattern of industry #1 as located only in Nation A while exporting #1 product to Nation B, and industry #2 located only in Nation B and exporting #2 product to Nation. According to the law of comparative advantage, employing all productive resources in both nations to this industrial geographical pattern will produce more total units of output of #1 and #2 available for use by all the inhabitants of both nations. In the absence of trade, if both nations would have factories producing #1 and # 2 products while fully employing all their respective productive resources, then the total production of #1 and #2 units will be less than the after trade totals. Thus, with free trade, there will be more total products available for the populations of both nations to consume. In classical theory analysis both nations gain from free trade as opposed to no trade.

In Ricardo's time, a nation's export industry was often associated with a nation's unique supply environment (e.g., availability of minerals deposits) and/or climate difference effects (e.g., on agricultural production) that resulted in differences in relative production costs between the nations. This comparative advantage argument for "free" trade is based on the notion of opening the domestic market to a foreign source which has lower labor time costs of production due to *supply productivity advantages not available in the domestic economy.*

In Ricardo's famous wine-cloth example, it was the climate that gave Portugal its absolute as well as its comparative advantage in production cost to Portugal's grapes and wine production. If the labor costs per hour in Portugal was much lower than in England in the mass production of cloth, then Portugal would have an absolute cost advantage in the production of cloth as well as wine. Nevertheless the law of comparative advantage would argue that all the cloth for the market in both countries should be produced in England, while Portugal produced all the wine for both countries since it had the greatest comparative cost advantage in the agricultural production of grapes.

Even if the production of both wine and cloth per unit of output was cheaper in Portugal than England, it would be beneficial for Portugal to concentrate its resources into the production of grapes to wine where it had the greatest real labor time cost advantage. Similarly even though it cost more to produce wine and cloth in England, the latter should use its resources in the production of cloth where it had the least cost disadvantage rather than allocating some of its resources to producing grapes for wine where the relative cost disadvantage in England was greater than in Portugal.

The result would be greater total production of wine and cloth for the same number of man hours worked in the two nations then if each nation produced both wine and cloth. This total supply increase due to free trade made possible an increase in the quantity of wine and cloth available to consumers in both England and Portugal.

In Ricardo's time, agricultural products and minerals were a very large share of total international trade. Divergences in production costs among nations due to climate and the non-random geographical distribution of natural resources were obviously significant. This meant that certain products were relatively cheaper to produce in one country than another. Consequently, Ricardo's law of comparative advantage was largely applicable for explaining free trade patterns between nations that would exist in the 19th century.

With the growth of mass production industries in the two centuries since Ricardo, however, mass production manufactured products makes up a larger portion of trade relative to minerals and agriculture than it did during Ricardo's time. The geographical location of industrial production is often determined on a somewhat different basis than comparative real costs in term of labor time necessary to produce a unit of output in any industry. In mass production manufacturing industries, differences in production costs among nations are not normally reflective of differences due to nature's climatic or mineral endowment associated with nation A vis-a-vis nation B. In mass production industries, the same technology typically is used in production of any particular product at any geographical location on earth. Accordingly, the amount of labor time per unit of manufacturing output is equal anywhere on the globe where a particular manufacturing industry is located. Differences in costs across nations in mass production manufacturing industries are primarily due to differences in the wage and fringe benefits costs per worker in one nation compared to the wages and fringe benefits cost for labor in another nation.

Keynes recognized this possibility when he wrote

> "A considerable degree of international specialization is necessary in a rational world in all cases where it is indicated by wide differences in climate, natural resources… But over an increasingly wide range of industrial products… Experience accumulates to prove that most modern mass production processes can be performed in most countries and climates with equal efficiency."[2]

Today, given the existence of multinational firms and the ease with which they can transfer technology internationally, any differences in relative costs of production in any particular industry is more likely to reflect national differences in money wages (per hour of labor) plus the costs of providing "civilized" working conditions such as a safe and healthy environment for workers, limiting the use of child labor, the costs to the enterprise of providing health insurance and pension benefits for employees, etc. Today in any free trade international system, where mass manufacturing and service industries are a significant portion of total trading volume among nations, global industrial trade patterns are more likely to reflect differences in wages, occupational safety and other labor expenses that the enterprise must bear, rather than real costs of production associated with either national differences in climate or difference in the availability of natural resources.

In the 21st century, low transportation and/or communication costs has made the delivery costs in providing many goods and services to distant foreign markets very low. Consequently, mass production industries that use low skilled workers, semi-skilled workers, or even, if available, high skilled workers are likely to locate in those nations where the economic system values human life the lowest, at least as measured by the compensation paid per hour of labor and the cost of the work environment provided workers.

Long ago most developed nations passed civilizing legislation that made unsafe "sweatshop" working conditions and the use of child labor illegal. More recently, enterprises in these developed nations have been made to bear the costs of not dumping pollution into the environment Yet such sweatshop, low wage and pollution conditions typically still exist in enterprise operating in most less developed nations. Consequently, the promotion of free trade competition among mass production industries favors the location of factories in nations that have little or no civilized regulations preventing sweatshop conditions, child labor use, wages below some legislative minimum, etc. This means that in developed nations with high paid workers and civilized workplace and pollution controls rules and regulations, free trade threatens the economic lives and civilized welfare conditions of workers and their families in developed nations. Mass production manufacturing facilities can be outsourced to these nations that still permit what the developed nations believe are uncivilized working and pollution conditions. The result has been that free trade has encouraged profit seeking multinational enterprises to shut down productive facilities in developed nations such as the United States and outsourcing labor demand to foreign nations contributing to domestic unemployment problems and wages stagnation or even decline.

On the other hand, in those domestic production processes where communication and/or transportation costs are very high and immigration legislation limited the importation of cheap labor (e.g., personal services such as servants, waiters, barbers, etc.) there cannot be any significant free trade foreign competition with domestic places of employment. Significant employment opportunities can still exist in these personal service industries of developed nations even though legislative regulations exist which require working condition standards, minimum wages, etc. Nevertheless, if free trade outsourcing displaces a growing number of workers from previously high paying mass production industries in developed nations, then the competition by displaced manufacturing workers for the remaining existing personal service jobs in non-tradeable production processes is likely to depress wages[3] in these activities, or at least prevent the wage of employed workers from rising significantly over time. It is, therefore, no wonder that the share of wages in United States gross domestic product has been declining in recent decades as the United States has engaged in more free trade agreements with nations that continue to have sweatshops manned by low paid workers.

As we crossed the threshold into the twenty-first century, Keynes's analytical framework indicated that the argument for complete free international trade as a means of promoting the wealth of all nations and their inhabitants cannot be rationalized on the ubiquitous application of the law of comparative advantage. Comparative advantage may still exist for minerals, agriculture and other industries where productivity is related to climatic conditions or mineral availability. Production in these climate and natural resource related industries, however, are often controlled by the market power of cartels and/or producer nations' governmental policies designed to prevent market prices from falling sufficiently to just cover the "real" costs of production associated with climate or natural resource availability. Those industries for which the law of comparative advantage might still be applicable are often largely sheltered from international competitive forces by cartel or government power. These industries reap monopoly rents over and above a competitive return on their production.

In the production of oil, for example, since the 1970s the OPEC cartel has created and maintained a large difference between the market price for crude oil and the costs of producing oil in countries such as Saudi Arabia and other middle eastern nations. Consequently the profits to the OPEC cartel including what economists call "monopoly rents" has, for decades, been very large. This cartel maintained price was so much greater than the potential cost of producing oil from shale that American and Canadian enterprises had an incentive to find ways to develop the technology for production of oil from shale and still make a significant more than competitive profit at the world price supported by the OPEC cartel. This new competition from shale oil has tended to reduce the cartel's control over price of oil significantly in recent years even though the price may be still much greater than the costs of production from oil wells in countries in the Middle East such as Saudi Arabia.[4]

The growth of multinational corporations in mass production industries and the movement towards a more liberalized free trading system in the final decades of the twentieth century encouraged business enterprises in developed nations to transfer their production technology in order to "outsource" production, i.e., to search for the lowest wage foreign workers available in order to reduce production costs and enhance corporate profits. The availability of "outsourcing" to cheap foreign labor also acts as a countervailing power to help corporations constrain any rising money wage cost for domestic workers organized by labor unions in developed countries.

Indeed in the early years of the 21st century, the rapidly developing industrial structure of many nations (e.g., China, India, Southeast Asia) can be largely attributed to the competitive search by multinational firms to utilize low wage foreign workers to compete with the high wage workers in developed nations to produce the identical goods and services under the same technological production processes. As suggested earlier, this outsourcing search for cheap foreign labor has created the equivalent of an "industrial reserve army" of workers in foreign nations that has constrained and sometimes even reduced the wages and living standards of workers in developed nations.

In the early decades after the second World war transportation and communication costs between nations was still significantly large. There was also national government restrictions on trade using tariffs and import quotas. In this environment, labor unions in mass production industries in developed economies could easily obtain increasingly high wages for the unionized workers. This brought about increasingly high domestic unit labor costs in developed nations which acted as a spur to encourage corporate managers to search for innovative domestic investment ways to improve domestic labor productivity and thereby reduce labor costs per unit of output. With the growth of multinationals and the removal of many restrictions on the international trading of mass produced manufactured goods, high domestic labor costs now are more likely to encourage managerial practices such as outsourcing, rather than encouraging investment in research and development to provide productivity enhancing new technology to lower unit labor production costs. Under current conditions, it is often cheaper to outsource using existing technical production processes overseas than incur the higher cost of searching for further technological improvements in production processes to reduce unit production costs in developed nations.

Consequently, the larger profits attributable to outsourcing have not been plowed back into as much research and technological development even if, in the long run, it is technological improvements in productivity that provide the basis for raising all living standards.

Under the rules of free trade today, there is less of an incentive for managers to pursue innovations to improve domestic labor productivity in any mass production industrial sector as long as inexpensive foreign labor can "do the job" with the existing technology and transportation and/or communication costs are relatively small. The decline in the rate of growth of domestic labor productivity in many developed nations since the 1970's can be, at least partly, related to this phenomena of emphasizing the use of cheap foreign labor vis-a-vis the search for domestic production process improvements by the private sector.

Except for production of some minerals and agricultural products, Post Keynesian analysis suggests that justification for the desirability of the expansion of international trade must be justified on the basis of increasing market demand globally. Demand driven expansion of trade can explain the growth of the wealth of nations in both the Adam Smith sense of exploiting economies of scale and in the sense of John Maynard Keynes who saw the lack of effective market demand as the main reason for the inability of modern economies to provide the full employment of resources income flow that they were capable of providing.

Nevertheless, rather than arguing that trade provides the opportunity for all nations to expand the effective market demand for the products they produce, defenders of free trade policies continually bring out the old chestnut of the classical theory's "law of comparative advantage" to justify "outsourcing" production by multinational firms in developed economies. These supporters of outsourcing claim that despite the obvious loss of the high wage jobs by American mass production workers to lower wage foreign workers, outsourcing is beneficial to both the United States economy and the rest of the world. They argue that, in the long run, free trade will result in more income and wealth for all nations by creating new higher value production jobs for workers in the developed nations who are freed from employment in lower value production processes by trade, as well as the creation of jobs in the nations to which production has been outsourced.

Unfortunately, the claim that outsourcing and free trade will create new high valued jobs in developed nations requires at least two classical assumptions that are not readily applicable to the real world in which we live. First, it is assumed that the hypothesized additional high value product that will be supplied as workers move from the outsourced production lines to the more (unspecified) higher valued product production automatically will create its own additional global demand for these additional high valued products. This assertion that additional supply always creates its own additional market demand merely is a reflection of the classical presumption that full employment in a free market always occurs. But as we have already noted Keynes demonstrated that to presume supply increases always creates its own demand increases to assure full employment could not be automatically applied to money-using entrepreneurial economies. Full employment is not an automatic outcome of free market competition domestically or internationally. Consequently, if there is anything the elite talking heads in the media should have learned since Keynes, it is that one cannot prove that there will automatically be gains from free trade to be shared by all trading economies unless one can be assured that there is full employment in all nations—before and after free trade.

That brings us to a second assumption required to make Ricardo's law of comparative advantage applicable to the real world in which we live. The textbook comparative advantage analysis assumes that the gains from trade occurs only if neither capital nor labor are mobile across national boundaries. If there is no capital or labor mobility across national boundaries, then the capital rich (developed) nations will specialize in industries that are most productive with a very capital intensive using technology, while the less developed region that has plenty of labor but little capital specializes in the labor intensive industries. This trade pattern of comparative advantage will use capital and labor in industries where the technology makes them most productive and therefore, by assumption, the total output globally will be maximized.

If capital is internationally mobile, however, and if, after trade, there is not global full employment, then these hypothetical benefits from free trade need not occur. With free international capital mobility and free trade, entrepreneurs will locate capital in the form of technologically advanced plant and equipment investments to produce goods in those nations where it is most profitable to produce, i.e., where units labor and workshop condition costs are lowest.[5] Thus, if multinational firms can shift technology from nation to nation, then it will take the same number of man-hours of input to produce a unit of output in each country—or as Keynes wrote "modern mass production processes can be performed in most countries...with equal efficiency".[6] Then the nation with cheap labor via lower money wage rates and fewer fringe benefits will have lower unit money labor costs for the production of manufactured items at all relevant ranges of production that the global market can absorb.

As long as the underdeveloped nation has an almost unlimited supply of cheap labor, the nation can attract enough foreign capital ultimately to produce all the manufactured goods necessary to meet global demand. In other words, as long as production with the latest technology does not run into significant diminishing returns and total after-trade market demand for all produced goods and services is not sufficient to assure global full employment, international production and trade patterns of mass production goods will be determined solely by absolute advantage of having a large supply of low cost workers available. The result will employment and living standards of the higher cost workers in developed nations will decline substantially.

The use of the classical comparative advantage analysis as a justification for letting free markets determine outsourcing, trade and international payments flows can be dangerous to the health of economies of developed nations especially those that restrict the use of child labor, provide their workers with civilized working conditions, and simultaneously provide a high wage standard of living. Such civilized nations will not have any absolute cost advantage in the production of tradeable goods and services vis-a-vis nations where sweatshop conditions including low wages prevail.

In sum, if capital is mobile internationally, as long as the underdeveloped nations have an absolute labor cost advantage in mass producing all tradeable goods because it has available a large additional supply of cheap labor, then the classical theory justification in claiming free trade agreements provides gains from trade for all nations is not applicable. Given abundant available cheap labor supply of unskilled and skilled workers, the less developed nations will attract foreign capital from the OECD nations to employ these workers to produce most, if not all, the tradeable goods and services that can be profitably sold globally. The developed nations will be left mainly with employment in industries that produce goods and services that are not tradable across national boundaries.

Of course, the proponents of free trade have an almost religious belief that despite the loss of high wage manufacturing jobs in developed nations due to outsourcing over recent years, the developed nations will develop (yet unspecified) higher skilled jobs in some advanced technology sector. The labor force in countries such as China and India will not have sufficient skills or education to be competitive in this forthcoming new technology high value product sector. Thus, the often heard comment that, in the long run, outsourcing is good for the developed economies with high cost labor forces assumes that unemployment will not be a significant problem as new, still unforeseen higher-skilled jobs will miraculously appear in developed nations such as the United States.

In his book describing the effect of outsourcing had on American workers at a factory Uchitelle[7] found that after two years only one out of three of these displaced workers ended up in a new job earning as much or slightly more than they had at their lost job. The other two thirds of the displaced workers earned significantly less or were still unemployed. Moreover most of these workers suffered severe damage to their self-esteem and to their mental health. In some cases this led to marriage breakups and other serious personal consequences.

Why did not most of these displaced workers find these new high value jobs that free trade advocates argues must be coming to America? The conventional wisdom is that it is the displaced workers' own fault for their being eligible only for lower paying less value productive jobs. An unemployed worker or a displaced worker needs only to pursue more education and they will always get a better job we are told without a smile on the face of the perpetrator of this innocent fraud! A call for better-educated workers as the remedy for workers displaced by outsourcing is a measure of a mind that has not thought through the problems of trade patterns in a freely trading global economy where child labor, unsafe working conditions, environmental damaging production, and a host of other factors that are devastating to the progress of a good civilized society.

Unless the governments of developed nations take deliberate action to secure and maintain full employment in their domestic economies, free trade has the potential to impoverish a significant portion of the population as unemployment rates in these countries remain high and those workers who are employed are forced to accept a real wage that is closer to being competitive to wages being paid to the abundant supply of unskilled and skilled workers in cheap foreign labor countries. Surely, politicians in developed nations should be made aware of these potential bad results that can occur from blindly applying the classical theory explanation of the benefits of free trade to today's problem of job outsourcing.

Notes

1. A. Smith, *An Inquiry Into The Wealth of Nations* (1776) reprinted in 1937 by Modern Library, New York.
2. J. M. Keynes, "National Self Sufficiency" [1933] reprinted in *The Collected Writings of John Maynard Keynes, 21*, edited by D. Moggridge (Macmillan, London, 1982), p. 238.
3. L. Uchitelle, *The Disposable American: Layoffs and Their Consequences*, (New York, Knopf, 2006).
4. This possibility was recognized in 1974 in a paper by P. Davidson, L. H. Falk and H. Lee "Oil: Its Time allocation and Project Independence" *Brookings Papers on Economic Activity, 2*, 1974 This paper is reprinted in *Inflation, Open Economies, and Resources; The Collected Writings of Paul Davidson, vol. 2* edited by L. Davidson (New York, New York University Press, 1991). The reference to shale is provided on p. 331 of the reprint edition.
5. Assuming transportation costs do not completely offset the lower labor costs per unit.
6. *Op.cit.*, p. 238.
7. L. Uchitelle, *The Disposable American: Layoffs and Their Consequences*, (New York, Knopf, 2006).

10

President Trump's Anti-free Trade Agreements Policy

In the 2016 election, President Trump received the support of many working class voters who were frustrated and even frightened by free trade agreements that encouraged the loss of domestic manufacturing factories and jobs to foreign nations who produce the same product with the same technology at a significantly lower money cost. As we have noted Uchitelle found displaced workers suffered mentally from the effects of outsourcing of their jobs, even if they were able to obtain other working positions. Obviously, then even for workers whose jobs had not yet been outsourced the potential threat to their self-esteem and standard of living provoked them to support of a candidate who promised to protect workers from further loss of factory and jobs due to free trade.

Candidate Trump recognized this discomfort of American blue collar workers and tapped into this frustration by promising to remove the US from free trade agreements that allowed this displacement of US factories and jobs. During the presidential campaign, Donald Trump promised that, if elected, he would not only stop further loss of factories and jobs, but he also promised he would also bring back these high wage jobs that had been outsourced.

Trumps basis of his anti free trade agreement proposal, however, was not based on the same principles as Keynes's attack on free trade in mass production manufacturing industries. Since President Trump has taken office, the US Trade Representative office has attempted to explain the basis of President Trump's anti-free trade agreement position in a report entitled "2017 Trade Policy Agenda".

Chapter 1 of the report indicates that President Trump believes that the "American people grew frustrated with our prior trade policy not because they ceased to believe in free trade and open markets, but because they did not see all the clear benefits from international trade agreements". The Trump Administration believes that the problem with past free trade agreements is that other nations practice "unfair trade practices" such as "unfair trade barriers to other markets that block US exports". Also that imports into US domestic product markets were being "distorted by dumped and/or subsidized imports" coming from other nations.

In general, the Trump administration believes the problem is that these existing free trade agreements do not promote truly free trade as foreign governments subsidize exports to sell their exports at less than their costs of production, while US exports are discriminated against in foreign markets.

Even if a portion of the large U.S. unfavorable balance of trade is due to these alleged conditions of subsidy, dumping and discrimination acts against US exports, as suggested in this report of the office of US Trade Representative, eliminating these "unfair" aspects of trade would still subject the United States to a large unfavorable balance of mass production industry trade because the labor costs of production in foreign nations are still so much lower than the labor costs in the United States for the same mass production products produced under the same technology in factories in less developed nations.

President Trump may have recognized the frustration of many American factory workers with the actual and/or potential effects of free trade agreements on their lives. Nevertheless, the Trump Administration has not zeroed on the fundamental economic cause—namely that workers in foreign factories are not protected by the United States civilized labor laws that cause United States located factories to have significantly larger money labor costs even though American workers are equally productively efficient as foreign factory workers using the same production process.

Even if the Trump Administration renegotiates and achieves trade agreements that prevent any foreign government subsidizing its export industries or discriminating via tariffs and/or quotas against the importation of products from the United States, it is questionable as to whether such Trump negotiated agreements will protect American workers jobs and incomes from product of foreign factories that are not required to remove all sweatshop conditions and pay equal money wages and fringe benefits per unit of output as American workers are legally entitled to when they are employed.

What this book has demonstrated is that only if policy decisions are based on a Keynes explanation of the operation of our money using, market oriented economic system, can a trade policy be developed to achieve the goals to protect the living standards of American factory workers.

This recommended trade policy is simple. Suppose the Chinese were to build a factory in California and operate it exactly as a similar factory located in China is operated—namely with child labor, uncivilized sweatshop conditions, wages at less than the minimum wage, etc. The United States labor laws would prohibit this California based factory to operate and sell any products in the United States. Consequently, the same restrictions should apply to factories outside the boundaries of the United States that operate in violation of US labor laws. After all, would the United States or any civilized nation permit imported products to be sold in domestic markets if the foreign factory employed slave labor?

Moreover the United States does not permit imports of pharmaceutical or food products that do not meet the legal standards of the US Food and Drug Administration to protect American consumers. Should not the United States government protect American workers by requiring foreign factories to meet the legal standards the government requires of factories located in the United States?

A simple trade policy would be to prevent importation of any products from foreign factories if those products and labor compensation and conditions did not meet the legal requirements that the United States imposed on entrepreneurs whose factories are located within the United States.

11

What Economic Policies Can a Democracy Adopt to Assure We Live in a Prosperous, Civilized Capitalist System?

A civilized society should encourage all its citizens to excel in all the endeavors they undertake. A civilized society must also provide its citizens with the opportunities to work to earn a decent income under civilized working conditions. A civilized society also should encourage the productive members of the community to maintain a sensitivity and compassion for the needs of others, and to have open and honest contractual dealing with everyone.

All these objectives are easier to obtain in a capitalist economic system where everyone has the opportunity to earn income. The ability to earn an honest day's income for an honest day's work creates self-esteem for the employed person and all the members of his/her household. Accordingly, government policies should be designed to assure enough market demand to make it profitable for enterprise to hire all members of society who want to work to earn income.

For the last four decades, however, the public debate over economic policy has been dominated by the belief that if self-interested individuals are permitted to operate in a free market without government interference and regulation, and without worrying about other less fortunate members of the community, the resulting free market will bring about an economic Utopia.

Yet the terrible 2007–2008 global financial crisis result came from deregulating financial institutions while permitting self-interest mortgage originators to encourage sub-prime borrowers to obtain a mortgage for a home they could not afford. Self-interest investment bankers then securitized these mortgages of subprime borrowers with a mix of more conventional mortgages and sold these mortgage backed derivatives with what later proved to be fraudulent claims that these derivative securities were as good as cash in terms of their liquidity. The result was a disaster not only for many sub-prime home owners who later found they could no longer afford their mortgage payments but also to the many innocent people who have lost jobs as the global economy sank into the Great Recession.

The purpose of this book has been to convince the reader that there is an alternative to the classical economic theory (1) that claimed that free markets are always the only way to make the economy beneficial to all members of society, and (2) that promoted the financial deregulation and the resulting market activity that brought on the Great Recession. This alternative Keynes-Post Keynesian theory provides a more realistic explanation of the operation of the market oriented entrepreneurial system in which we live. This alternative explanation also can provide guidelines on how to cure the flaws that remain in this market-oriented, entrepreneurial system without destroying the good things that are delivered by our money using, market oriented economic system. The preceding chapters have indicated how Keynes's explanation of the operation of our economic system demonstrates that to produce prosperity for all, government can and must assure that private sector employers have sufficient profit incentives to employ all workers who are actively seeking employment.

Franklin Roosevelt was the first President to recognize the power of Keynes's philosophy that government has a positive powerful role to play as buyer of last resort to provide employment and prosperity to all its citizens. Although Roosevelt was still hampered by fears of a national debt overwhelming the nation, when the Second World War broke out such fears were brushed aside. Spending sufficiently to assure the winning of the war financed by huge government deficits proved beyond a shadow of a doubt that the government could always play an active role in guaranteeing full employment prosperity for its business enterprises and its labor force. If there is sufficient market demand for their products, even if available workers lack sufficient skill for a particular job, this is not an unsurmountable problem. All that is required is sufficient market demand to make it profitable to provide on-the-job training.

Republican and Democratic successors to Roosevelt adopted variations of Keynes's policy initiatives to maintain economic prosperity, even if they did not necessarily recognize that these policy prescriptions were first suggested by Keynes. As we have already noted, President Truman's Administration produced the Marshall Plan where the United States as the major international trade surplus nation used its wealth to solve the post war trade imbalance problem The Marshall Plan created job opportunities in export industries for American workers while also helping the European nations, whether they were allies or former enemies, to feed their populations and rebuild their national economies.

President Eisenhower succeeded Truman to the presidency. Eisenhower instituted one of the largest peacetime public works programs ever undertaken, the building of the interstate highway system. Not only did construction of the interstate highway system create profits and jobs in the construction and related industries, but it also provided the nation with a transportation system that increased the productivity of American factories by making it less expensive to take delivery of raw materials at the factory door and less expensive to deliver the finished product to the marketplace. The result of such active government policies was to make the United States and most of the free world a more prosperous and civilized place in which to live.

Meanwhile, during these years the Federal Reserve recognized that its primary function was to maintain the liquidity and stability of financial markets, while at the same time the Glass Steagall Act was strictly enforced so that the banking function of making non-resalable loans to customers was legally separated from the underwriting function of investment bankers to sell securities in well organized financial markets.

With the advent of Stagflation in the 1970s and the victory of the classical free market philosophy over the perverted view of Keynesianism that appeared in textbooks such as written by Paul Samuelson after the Second World War, central banks and governments began to adopt a different, less civilized philosophical policy approach, to the economy. In 1979, for example, after a second spike in crude oil prices engineered by OPEC, the Federal Reserve, under Chairman Paul Volker, raised interest rates to double digit levels to deliberately destroy profit opportunities for many businesses and to create the highest unemployment rate since the Great Depression. This policy did stop the wage price inflation process in its tracks—but at a great cost to enterprise and American workers.

In the 1970s, the OPEC cartel of oil producing countries exercised its power to raise the world price of crude oil. This caused inflation in the oil importing developed nations and depressed their economies. Since many union wage contacts in American industries had cost of living clauses, the OPEC oil price increase resulted in unionized workers receiving cost of living increases in their money wages. These cost of living wage increases created additional upward pressures on the price level and inflation became a major threat to the economy. As we have already noted, at this time, the Federal Reserve under Chairman Volker raised the interest rate to double digit level to fight inflation. The result was the economy stagnated while inflationary forces still pressed for a while on the price level. This condition was called Stagflation.

Ultimately a depressed economy plus the start of new non OPEC crude oil supplies coming onto the markets from regions such as the North Sea, and Alaska reduced the market power of the OPEC cartel put OPEC less in the control of the market price.

The lesson taken away from this 1979–1981 Federal Reserve induced stagflation episode of a deliberate policy to create high unemployment to end an inflationary period where wage incomes inflation was exacerbating the initial OPEC cartel inflation. It seemed to fit the philosophy of classical economic theory. An independent central bank board of governors, whose members were not subject to political elections every two years, could make independent tight monetary policies that the public would have to accept, even though the results of collapsing profit opportunities and a large increase in unemployment devastated many members of the population. It was recognized that central bank tight money policies would be aimed at constraining inflationary forces that are unleashed when the economy becomes so prosperous that workers and managers believe that, in a free market, they can raise wages and prices without losing customers.

This classical economic theory suggested that central bank policy should and would be designed so that if the inflation rate was larger than the central bankers believed desirable, then the central bank had the responsibility to institute a high interest rate, tight money policy deliberately aimed at producing fewer profit opportunities for business firms. This would induce employers to lay off many workers. The result was to make workers and their unions more docile and willing to accept unchanged wages or even falling money wage rates. Monetary policy since then was often seen as "the only game in town" to control inflation and unemployment levels.

Andrew Mellon's classical theory's philosophical message to President Hoover was back in the corridors of power. When the Great Depression began, President Hoover indicated he wanted to take some positive action to end the depression. Hoover's Secretary of the Treasury, Andrew Mellon, cautioned against government action. In his memoir, President Hoover wrote: "Mr. Mellon had only one formula. Liquidate labor, liquidate stocks, liquidate the farmer, liquidate real estate. It will purge the rottenness out of the system…People will work harder, lead a more moral life."[1]

In the 1970s, to purge the stagflation rottenness out of the system (i.e., high incomes inflation) required liquidating business' and workers' income earning opportunities. With this loss of income opportunities, it was believed that enterprise and workers would work harder and demand less when a job opportunity or profit opportunity, in the long run, does reappear. Surely this Mellon philosophy approach is not a civilized solution to the economic problems of a twenty first century capitalist system.

A Keynes solution is certainly more civilized and simple. As long as people wanted to work, the government must make sure that they have an opportunity to obtain a job fitting to their skills and, if necessary, obtain new skills by way of on-the-job training. If, there is sufficient demand from private sector buyers to create market demand for all the goods and services that the nation's business firms can produce with a fully employed labor force, than the government's only responsibility is to make sure that employers are obeying the laws that a civilized society enacts to ensure safe working conditions, product safety requirements, etc. In addition government must introduce an incomes policy that restricts increases in money wages to increases in labor productivity.

If, and only if, there is a significant short fall in market demand for products of the nation's industries, then the government should take an active role in pumping up market demand to create profit opportunities for businesses and job opportunities for the otherwise unemployed. When a significantly large recession appears on the economic horizon and private sector buyers remain reluctant to spend additional sums, then the government must step in to act as the purchaser of last resort.

Keynes argued that the government should attempt to spend in those areas that are investments in productivity enhancing activities that will provide useful goods and services for the population. If government spending appears to be "the only means of securing an approximation to full employment...this need not exclude all manner of compromises and devises by which the public authority will co-operate with private initiative."[2]

Accordingly government financing of the rebuilding of the economic infrastructure by building and repairing the nation's highways, bridges, airports, harbors are clearly productive investments that can be accomplished by government letting contracts to private enterprise.[3] Other infrastructure projects that would contribute to improving the health and therefore the productive life of the nation's citizens include the repair and improvement of water supply system, and sanitary facilities of all kinds. Spending to develop light rail transportation systems to promote moving commuter traffic to reliable public transportation will reduce the use of automobiles that often clog our city streets and highways. Such projects will also contribute to the nation's effort to prevent global warming and reduce the pollution of the atmosphere that we leave to our children and grandchildren.

Government spending on better education for all its citizens is obviously desirable as an investment in making our system a more civilized one with a skilled and intelligent population. This spending to provide a better useful education can take many forms. In the 1930s, for example, President Roosevelt created the Civilian Conservation Corps (CCC). This institution took unemployed young men off the streets of the cities and moved then to areas like Appalachia where they were housed and fed. In the Appalachian forests, these young men were taught to do jobs requiring some skills such as building houses, roads and parks, etc. The result was a labor force that was educated to do many crafts that would be demanded as the economy recovered from the Great Depression.

In our high tech global economy of the twenty first century, education is an especially important investment project for developing the skills, knowledge, and pleasures of future generations. With local governments incurring significant shortfalls in their tax receipts, local governments finds it difficult, if not impossible, to even maintain the present educational system, much less upgrade the educational system. If the federal government would provide funding for local and state educational systems, our public schools, public community colleges, and public universities could become the platform for launching our citizens into a more productive life.

Government spending can also encourage research and development by universities and private sector business firms for better products and for new procedures to better protect the population from diseases.

If, however, Keynes warned "we are so sensible…taking careful thought before we add to the 'financial' burdens of prosperity by building for them [productive investment for them to use, then]… we have no such easy escape from the sufferings of unemployment."[4] Those who argue that the government should not borrow to create jobs and productive investments for future generations to use, because the borrowing will impoverish future generations with government debts, do not realize how much we will impoverish future generations by not providing these productive outcomes if the government does nothing in order to pass on a smaller national debt to posterity.

Clearly, the list of possible investment projects that government can encourage with a significant spending recovery plan is enormous. Many of these projects would be desirable to invest in even if the economy was not in a significant recession. The opportunities for improving the productivity of our citizens are too obvious to not take advantage of them because of the argument that the resulting national debt will be too burdensome for our children.

Probably an important, but potentially politically controversial, project involves investing in the health care for all the citizens of the nation. Unlike most developed nations, until 2014 the United States did not have any national health program to protect the health of all its citizens. Instead, it relied on, and still relies on, a patchwork of various health insurance programs, which gained even more force with the passage of the Affordable Care Act, i.e., Obamacare.

During the Second World War, many employers provided fringe benefits such as health insurance plans to recruit workers. These private health insurance plans for workers financed by employers have been the major form of national health insurance for decades. This way of providing health insurance adds significantly to the business firm's costs of producing and selling its products. It has been suggested that for the Big Three United States automakers, the cost of health care for their employees and retirees (whose health care costs are also covered) per automobile produced is greater than the cost of steel used to in producing automobiles. This clearly puts United States employers at a tremendous competitive cost disadvantage relative to producing cars in foreign nations especially in an era where free international trade is being foisted on the public.

All retired workers who are over 65 years of age may be covered by the government's Medicare health plan. For households whose workers are not covered by employee health insurance plans and for those unemployed for any length of time, the only way to obtain health care coverage is to purchase private health insurance. Statistics indicate that before Obamacare millions of Americans were without any health plan coverage and therefore did not go to doctors for preventive medicine. At least since Obamacare in 2014, all residents of the United States should have some form of medical insurance, although the costs of administrating these many different plans (and therefore the income of those administrating these plans) are significantly greater than the costs associated with administering a single payer system such as Medicare.

It should be obvious that to participate and flourish in our economic system access to health care is a priority. Good health increases productivity and longevity. As Stephen P. Dunn, a senior strategy advisor to the English Department of Health and Director of Provider Development of the National Health Service East of England, states: "Reduction in avoidable disease and increases in the years of healthy life expectancy would accelerate economic growth… The economic loss to society of shortened lives due to early death and chronic disability is hundreds of billions of dollars per year."[5]

An important idea that a civilized society should face is that health care is more than a basic right for every member of the community. If every person is going to effectively contribute to the productive activities of the nation, and if this contribution is to be done well, then the individual and the members of his/her family must be as healthy as the practice and technological advances of medicine permits.

A civilized society recognizes the basic right of all its member to find employment where they can use their talents to turn out the best possible product. Surely there is an argument to consider whether access to health care, paid by the community at large rather by employers and individuals can improve the productivity of workers and thereby benefit the community. For healthier workers are always more productive workers. Keynes does not have a facile solution to the question of whether all members of society are entitled to health care independent of their income. But surely there is some evidence which indicates that access to universal health care independent of a family's income would be a productive investment for society to undertake.

In sum, there are a significantly large number of investment projects that government can finance by spending to encourage the private sector to produce results. The problem is not a shortage of financing; the problem is often a shortage of political resolve to take on such productive spending policies by government.

Finally we have hopefully demonstrated to our readers that government regulators have an important role to play in assuring the members of our society that public financial markets are well organized and orderly. Furthermore participants in financial market should be required to provide contracts that deal fairly and honestly with other participants. This will protect households who are searching for financial assets to place their savings in order to meet any future spending plans (whether anticipated or not) during their active income earning period plus provide sufficient liquid purchasing power in their retirement years.

The task of putting our Keynes-Post Keynesian solution into practice will not be easy. It, however, offers more hope for a stable prosperous economic system than the efficient market philosophy of classical economic theory that has been promoted in recent decades. The latter has brought us again to the brink of economic disaster. We can only hope the public and our politicians can only learn from this book that there are better ways of achieving a good economic life for all citizens than merely trusting to a free market to solve our problems.

Notes

1. H. Hoover, *The Memoirs of Herbert Hoover, The Great Depression 1929–1941* (Macmillan, New York, 1952), p. 30.
2. J. M. Keynes, *The General Theory of Employment Interest and Money* (London, Macmillan, 1936), p. 378.
3. Statistics indicate that in America there are a large number of bridges and highways that have are urgently in need of repair.
4. *Op. Cit.*, p. 131.
5. S. P. Dunn, *TheUncertain Foundation of Post Keynesian Economics,* (London, Routledge, 2008), p. 187.

Index

A

Affordable Care Act (Obamacare) 152
Age of Reason 11
Arrow, Kenneth 25
Astronomy, probability approach 28
Auction-rate securities markets 81, 82, 89
Austerity programs 78, 108, 112, 118
Axioms 12

B

Bank runs 121
Bankruptcy 46
Barter economy 15, 34, 41
Bear Stearns 87–88
Berlin Wall, construction of 110
Bernanke, Ben 99
Blanchard, Oliver 32
Bottlenecks 63, 64, 66
Bretton Woods 104–111, 120

Britain 63
Broker-dealers 82
Buffer stocks 69, 70, 71
Bush, George H.W. 94

C

Capital controls 120, 121–122
Capitalism, civilized 145–154
CCC 151
CDS 81, 84, 85
Central banks 86
　globalization 115–116, 121–122, 123
　inflation 64–66, 74, 148–149
　interest rates 56
　and known future 27
　and liquidity 5, 48, 88
　neutral money axiom 32–33
　quantitative easing 94
China 99–103, 120
Chinese Communist party 100

Churchill, Winston 23
"Circuit breakers" 48, 86
Civilian Conservation Corps. *See* CCC
Classical theory 24–36
  on China 100
  domination of 19
  exchange rates 102–103
  on free competition 20–23
  gross substitution 35, 36
  international trade 104, 112, 128, 130, 136, 138
  "known future" assumption 25–31, 45, 57
  liquidation 149
  neutral money 31–35
  on regulation 15, 127
  saving 40, 41, 50, 52
  sub classifications 7, 8, 13–14, 15
  unemployment 16, 22–23, 31, 48, 49
Clinton, Bill 112, 113
Closed, double-entry bookkeeping 115
Closed economy model 97
Columbia University 8
Commodity prices 67, 68, 69, 71
Communism 108
Comparative advantage analysis 127, 128–134, 136, 138
Consumption spending 42, 51, 52, 53, 108
Contractionism 105
Contractual obligations 14, 15, 34, 43–46, 58, 100
Credit card debt 56
Credit default swaps. *See* CDS

Cross border fund movements 116, 122

D
Dawes Plan 106
Debreu, Gerard 25
Debt certificates 3
"Deficit hawks" 58
Deficit spending 52, 55, 56–62
Deflation 67, 69, 70, 73
Democracy 23, 72, 145–154
Deregulation 10, 25, 146
Desert Storm 70
Diminishing returns in production 63, 64, 65, 66, 129
Direct foreign investment spending 117, 118, 123
Dissaving 50, 52–53, 55, 61, 65
Dot.com bubble 59
Dunn, Stephen P. 153
Durable assets, 17n1, 36, 42, 47, 48, 51, 68

E
Economic growth rates 32, 64, 99
Education 53, 139, 150, 151
Efficient market theory 29, 82, 83–85, 89, 90, 102, 103
Einstein, Albert, general theory of relativity 34
Eisenhower, Dwight D. 61, 147
Elizabeth II, Queen 1
Employment, full
  creation of 55–62
  in free market 21–23, 31, 51, 137
  global 103–104, 116, 117, 140

government regulation 35
and inflation 63–78
market demand 40, 42, 52, 53, 136, 147, 150
and savings 36, 50, 51
Enlightenment 11
Entrepreneurial system
and employment 16, 22, 31, 35, 40, 49, 61, 62, 66, 67
forward contracts 68
free trade agreements 128, 137, 144
inflation 74
monetary policy stimulus 56
money contracts 43, 44
European Union 114, 118
Exchange rates 102–105, 122, 123
Expansionism 105
Exports
after Second World War 106–110
domestic employment 97, 98–103
free trade agreements 127–140, 141–144
International Money Clearing Union 116–117, 119, 120
Marshall Plan 147

F

Federal debt 61
Federal Reserve
after 9/11 86, 88
and Bear Stearns 87–88
interest rate 56, 103, 148, 149
liquidity 147
Quantitative Easing 33, 94–95
Financial markets
and liquidity 81–95

regulation of 90–95
First World War 59
Fischer, Stanley 113
Flight capital 120, 121
Foreign reserves 48, 99, 106, 116
Forward contracts 14, 68
Forward market price (short-run price) 66, 67, 69
Free exchange markets 120, 121
Free market pricing model 21
Free market theory 7, 10, 11, 20
Free trade agreements 127–140, 141–144
Friedman, Milton 7, 17n1, 32, 33, 50, 51, 52
Fully liquid assets 48

G

G-7 nations 113
Galbraith, John K. 34, 72
Geographical location of industry 73, 129–131
Glass Steagall Act 94, 147
Global financial crisis 2007/2008
and deregulation 10
interest rates 56
long term debt investments 83, 84
as unforeseen 1–6, 9–11, 20, 27
Globalization 97–124
Bretton Woods 104–111
and free trade 73, 75–78
International Monetary Clearing Union 115–124
international payments system 111, 112–114
Goldman Sachs 87, 89, 90
Gold reserves 110, 111

Gold window 111
Government regulation 27, 28, 29, 30, 35
Great Depression 2, 59, 60, 72, 149
"Great Recession" 19, 56
Greenspan, Alan 10–11, 13, 17, 19, 20, 21, 25, 81
Gross substitution axiom 35, 36
G-7 nations 113

H

Harrod, Roy 41
Health care 152–153
Hicks, Sir John 30
Hilsenrath, J. and Rappaport, L. 33
Home Owners Loan Association (HOLC) 94
Hoover, Herbert 149
House Oversight and Government Reform Committee 10, 11

I

Iceland, banking system 114
Illiquidity 3, 4, 44, 48, 86–88, 90–92, 94
IMCU 115–124
  rules 122–124
IMF 107–108, 113, 119
Imports 57, 97, 98–103, 105–110, 117–120, 143, 148
  quotas 135, 143
Incomes inflation 64, 67, 68, 71–73, 75, 77
Incomes policy 68, 72–78
Income tax, personal 56, 57
India 99

Industrialization 72, 73, 75, 76, 77, 78, 135
Inequality, economic 8, 23, 61, 76
Inflation
  and full employment 63–78
  globalization and 102, 103
  and IMCU 123
  OPEC and 148
  Quantity Theory of Money 32, 33
  quantitative easing 33
  production costs 63, 66
  role of central bank 65, 66, 148, 149
Infrastructure 150–152
Interest rates 55, 56, 66, 103, 148, 149
International Clearing Agency, 124n8
International Monetary Clearing Union. *See* IMCU
International Monetary Fund. *See* IMF
International payments system 111–114. *See also* IMCU
Iraq 70

J

Jackson, Andrew 59
Japan 99
Johnson, Lyndon B. 61
J. P. Morgan Chase 87–88

K

Kennedy, John F. 61
Keynes, John Maynard
  on classical theory 16, 29, 30
  on efficiency 138

on faults in economic system 23
The General Theory of Employment, Interest and Money 8, 34, 35
on Great Depression 2
and inflation 64–65
on international payments system 112
on international specialization 132
Keynes Plan 104–111, 114
liquidity preference theory 82, 85
on market demand 136
on monetary stimulus 56
on money 45
on money contracts 15
on power of economists 19
on real exchange economy 33, 34
on saving 36, 42–43, 52
Treatise on Money 67
on unemployment 42, 48, 49–50, 52, 65, 151
Keynes Plan 104–111, 114
"Known future" assumption 13, 14, 24–31, 34, 51, 84
Krugman, Paul 8

L

Labor costs 22, 64, 68, 71, 130, 142, 143
foreign 78, 135, 136, 138
Labor hiring contract 68
Labor unions 22, 23, 72, 74, 135, 148, 149
Laissez-faire system 28, 30, 73, 106, 112
Liquid assets 2, 3–4
and financial crisis 9
fully liquid assets 48
globalization 100, 110–111, 121
and savings 36, 46–53
Liquidity
crisis of 4, 5
employment 43–46
financial markets 81–95
Keynes on 14, 15, 49–50, 52
regulation 90–95
and unemployment 65
Liquidity preference theory 82, 85
London School of Economics (LSE) 1
Long Term Capital Management (LTCM) 112, 113
Lucas, Robert 7, 26

M

Malaysia 112
Market demand, expansion of 55, 128, 129
Market "fundamentals," analysis of 82, 83–84
Market makers 83, 86, 88
of last resort 48
Marshall, Alfred 67
Marshall Plan 108, 109, 111, 147
Marx, Karl 73
Massachusetts Institute of Technology 7
Mellon, Andrew 149
Mexico 112
Middle class, expansion of 61
Minimum wage legislation 22, 23, 143
Modern probability theory (stochastic theory) 26
Money 19–36
and civil law of contracts 44
gross substitution 35, 36

Keynes on 49
"known future" assumption 24–31
neutral money 31–35
supply 32
Money contracts 15, 43–45, 47, 52, 58, 66
Money wages
  free trade agreements 132, 135, 138, 143
  and inflation 64, 65, 68, 71–75, 123, 148, 149
  and unemployment 22, 23, 49, 50
Monopoly rents 134
Moore, G.E. 41
Mortgage backed derivatives 3, 4, 9, 14, 29, 33, 87, 146

N
National debt 58–61, 62, 146, 151, 152
Neoclassical Synthesis Keynesianism 7, 13
Neutral money axiom 31, 32–34, 51, 64
"New Deal" 60
New Keynesianism 8
New York Federal Reserve Bank 112, 113
New York Stock Exchange 87
  collapse 1929 2
New York Times 89, 90
9/11 86, 87, 88
Nixon, Richard 111
Nobel Prize 21

O
Obama, Barack 113
  stimulus spending plan 98, 120

Obamacare (Affordable Care Act) 152
OECD nations 75, 139
Oil supplies 70, 134, 148
OPEC 134, 148
Outsourcing 8, 75–77, 133, 135–137, 139, 141

P
Pentagon, terrorist attack 86
Post Keynesianism 2, 5–6, 8, 9
  entrepreneurial system 146
  globalization 101, 102, 136
  liquidity theory 14–15
  tax reduction 57
  unemployment 65
  "unknown future" assumption 45
"price talk" 89
Princeton University 8
Probability distribution 26–31, 84
Production costs and inflation 63, 66, 71, 129–131, 135
Productivity
  free trade agreements 128, 130, 134, 135–136
  health 152, 153
  and incomes inflation 68, 71, 72, 75–77
  increased 3, 64, 65
  and inflation 123
  infrastructure 147, 150
Public services 40

Q
"Quantitative Easing" (QE) 33, 94–95
Quantity Theory of Money 31, 32, 64

Rating agencies 4, 92
Rational expectations theory 26–27, 45, 57, 95n3
"Real" contracts 15, 25, 41
Real exchange economy 33, 34
Recession 40, 52–53, 59, 60, 77, 121, 150. *See also* "Great Recession"
Resolution Trust Corporation (RTC) 88, 94
Revolutionary War, US 58
Ricardo, David 128, 129, 130–131
Risk management 10, 11, 20, 21
Roosevelt, Franklin D. 59, 60, 146, 151
Rubin, Robert 112
Russia 112, 113

Samuelson, Paul 7, 13
  Foundations of Economic Analysis, 17n2
Sargent, Thomas 27
Savings
  in classical theory 40, 41, 50, 52
  from current income 36, 45, 51
  Friedman on 51, 52
  Keynes on 36, 42–43, 52
  and liquidity 46–50
  return on 4
Savings and Loan banks (S & L) insolvency crisis 88
Scholes, Myron 113
Securities Act 1933 90
Second World War
  European imports 105, 106–108
  health care 152
  national debt 60, 61
  training 53
  unemployment and conscription 60
Securities and Exchange Commission (SEC) 90, 91–94, 121
Securitization 4, 91, 93
Self-interest 10, 14, 15, 20–21, 24–26, 74, 145–146
Short-run price. *See* Forward market price
Smith, Adam 128, 136
Solow, Robert 7
"Specialists," stock exchange 82, 83
Spot markets 25, 66–70
Stagflation 8, 148, 149
Stiglitz, Joseph 8
Stochastic theory. *See* Modern probability theory
Stock market bubble 1920s 59
Subprime mortgage derivatives 114
Subprime mortgages 4, 9, 81, 146
Summers, Lawrence 29, 83
Supranational Central Bank 114
Suspension of trading, temporary 86
Sweatshops 132, 133, 134, 138, 143
Switzerland, banking system 114

Taxation, corporate 76
Tax-based incomes policy (TIP) 76–77
Thailand, currency crisis 112
Thatcher, Margaret 74
Toxic assets 4, 5, 95
Trade deficit 99, 101, 102, 103, 106–108, 119
Truman, Harry 108, 147

Trump, Donald 141–144

U
Uchitelle, L. 139
Unemployment 39–53
 cause of 40, 55
 classical theory 16, 22–23, 31, 48, 49
 European 77
 historical 59–60
 Keynes on 42, 48, 49–50, 52, 65, 151
 natural rate of 75
 and market demand 40, 49, 53, 55, 58
Unemployment benefits, reduction of 75
United States Federal Reserve System 115
United States Securities and Exchange Commission 90, 91–94, 121
United States (US)
 and Mexico 112
 foreign borrowing 99
 international payments 110
 and Second World War 106–108

strategic petroleum reserves 70
surplus merchandise trade balance 109
unfavorable balance of trade 98, 142
University of Chicago 7, 26
"Unknown future" 44, 45, 81, 85
US Food and Drug Administration 143

V
Vietnam War 61
Volker, Chairman 148

W
Wall Street Journal 33, 87
Walrasian analysis 30, 31, 34
Walras, Leon 25
Weintraub, Sidney 76–77
White, Harry Dexter 107–108
Working conditions, civilized 132–133, 138
World Bank 107, 108, 119
World Trade Center 86, 87